Cambridge Elements

Elements in Historical Theory and Practice
edited by
Daniel Woolf
Queen's University, Ontario

KNOWLEDGE AND NARRATIVE

Chiel van den Akker
Vrije Universiteit Amsterdam

Shaftesbury Road, Cambridge CB2 8EA, United Kingdom

One Liberty Plaza, 20th Floor, New York, NY 10006, USA

477 Williamstown Road, Port Melbourne, VIC 3207, Australia

314–321, 3rd Floor, Plot 3, Splendor Forum, Jasola District Centre, New Delhi – 110025, India

103 Penang Road, #05–06/07, Visioncrest Commercial, Singapore 238467

Cambridge University Press is part of Cambridge University Press & Assessment, a department of the University of Cambridge.

We share the University's mission to contribute to society through the pursuit of education, learning and research at the highest international levels of excellence.

www.cambridge.org
Information on this title: www.cambridge.org/9781009539715

DOI: 10.1017/9781009103961

© Chiel van den Akker 2025

This publication is in copyright. Subject to statutory exception and to the provisions of relevant collective licensing agreements, no reproduction of any part may take place without the written permission of Cambridge University Press & Assessment.

When citing this work, please include a reference to the DOI 10.1017/9781009103961

First published 2025

A catalogue record for this publication is available from the British Library

ISBN 978-1-009-53971-5 Hardback
ISBN 978-1-009-10834-8 Paperback
ISSN 2634-8616 (online)
ISSN 2634-8608 (print)

Cambridge University Press & Assessment has no responsibility for the persistence or accuracy of URLs for external or third-party internet websites referred to in this publication and does not guarantee that any content on such websites is, or will remain, accurate or appropriate.

For EU product safety concerns, contact us at Calle de José Abascal, 56, 1°, 28003 Madrid, Spain, or email eugpsr@cambridge.org

Knowledge and Narrative

Elements in Historical Theory and Practice

DOI: 10.1017/9781009103961
First published online: November 2025

Chiel van den Akker
Vrije Universiteit Amsterdam

Author for correspondence: Chiel van den Akker, c.m.vanden.akker@vu.nl

Abstract: This Element is concerned with narrative as a mode of knowing. It draws attention to the epistemic value of historical narrative qua narrative. This it does not only in an abstract sense, but also with the help of recent works of history. Special attention is given to narrative sentences and narrative theses. A narrative thesis redescribes the actions and events the historian is concerned with and allows for the temporal whole or unity we associate with narrative, with its beginning, middle, and end. A thesis, it is argued, is indispensable and qualifies the work of historians as narrative.

The concern with narrative has not lost any of its relevance, for the simple reason that it informs us about history as an academic discipline and the knowledge it produces. For as long as historians decide what events are important in their past and for what reason, they will rely on narrative.

Keywords: narrative knowledge, narrative sentences, narrative theses, epistemic value, history

© Chiel van den Akker 2025

ISBNs: 9781009539715 (HB), 9781009108348 (PB), 9781009103961 (OC)
ISSNs: 2634-8616 (online), 2634-8608 (print)

Contents

Preface	1
1 Narrative's Indispensability	8
2 Narrative Sentences	17
3 Narrative Theses	32
Epilogue	53
Bibliography	57

Preface

> Historians may be wiser than they can say, but only if we hear what they have to tell.
>
> ____Louis Mink

At the end of the *Odyssey*, Odysseus is greatly alarmed by Penelope's suitors who were able to arm themselves. Apparently, someone left the door of the armory open, providing them with the opportunity. Odysseus is informed by his son Telemachus that it was his mistake:

> and no one else is to blame.
> I left the door of the room, which can close tightly,
> open at an angle.[1]

Telemachus accepts responsibility – blame – for his action, even though he did not intend to leave the door open. But the consequences of his deed, and the suffering it causes, he realizes, are his. This realization of what has unintentionally been brought about is, Aristotle holds, a typical narrative feature, an element of its *muthos*, as the hero comes to know the harm he has done, and of what he had been ignorant, reversing how he views his deeds.[2] It strengthens the audience's involvement in the story and their sympathy toward its protagonists.

For some deed to be an action, it must be intentional under one of its descriptions:[3] Telemachus rushed to the armory to arm himself and his father; but we just as easily describe the same deed in terms of which it is unintentional: Telemachus left the door open; or in any other way: Telemachus made a mistake, and: Penelope's suitors were able to arm themselves. Mistakes are actions too, albeit ones that do not bring about what the actor intended. The description we use depends on the purpose we want it to serve. This includes describing the deed in terms unacceptable and unavailable to the actor, although we are morally obligated not to undo the deed in any of its descriptions. The door of the room will remain left open, however we decide to describe the deed. Usually, a series of descriptions is used to capture the action and the good or harm it did, with *narrative* being the structure that makes the action and its consequences intelligible, affording the sort of practical wisdom – *phronēsis*, as Aristotle calls it – that cannot be found elsewhere.

---

[1] *Odyssey* 22, 154. Translation by Williams, *Shame*, 50.
[2] Aristotle, *Poetics*, 52a29. For an introduction to this text, which is simultaneously an introduction to narrative theory, see Kent Puckett, *Narrative Theory*, 24ff.
[3] Davidson, "Agency," 45–46.

Although the concept of action not necessarily requires narrative, despite what some authors think, we do have a much better understanding of the suitors armoring themselves and of Odysseus being alarmed by it when we come across these actions in the epic, albeit that each of these actions is intelligible without it. Often an action suggests that there is a story to tell. Leaving the door of the armory open creates the sort of suspense and demand for resolve that are typical of narrative. It is the concept of action in connection to narrative that interests us here. This connection is not incidental, and it has been philosophically thematized ever since Aristotle's treatise on poetics. It also is a central concern in the debate on narrative as a *mode of knowing* in the philosophy of history, which is what this Element is about. Historians are concerned with actions and sufferings, relative to the societal changes they study. An action is but one feature of narrative. What happens to its protagonists, and the setting of their actions and sufferings, are each variously more or less prominent elements of any narrative as well, including historical narrative.[4] Before turning to narrative as a mode of knowing in the discipline of history, I will make a few further prefatory remarks on the conceptions of action and narrative, and their connection. Some readers might want to turn to the first Section 1 directly.

Discussing the concept of action in the context of ancient Greek epic and tragedy, Bernard Williams discerns four of its key features. He writes:

> Everywhere, human beings act, and their actions cause things to happen, and sometimes they intend those things, and sometimes they do not; everywhere, what is brought about is sometimes to be regretted or deplored, by the agent or by others who suffer from it or by both; and when that is so, there may be a demand for some response from that agent, a demand made by himself, by others, or by both.[5]

Cause, intention, state, and response are the elements of action. The action here is not a basic action such as opening a door, but a complex action, such as leaving the door of the armory open, and the wider context in which it is to be situated. The demand for response ties the concept of action to that of responsibility. This connection is often thematized in narrative. It is one of the practical lessons that narrative teaches: "the responsibilities we have to recognize extend in many ways beyond our normal purposes and what we intentionally do."[6] An action, Williams notes,

---

[4] Megill, "Recounting the Past: Description, Explanation, and Narrative in Historiography," 627–653, at 644–645.
[5] Williams, *Shame*, 55. Williams shows that the Greek sense of action and responsibility is close to our own.
[6] Williams, *Shame*, 74.

stands between the inner world of disposition, feeling and decision and an outer world of harm and wrong. *What I have done* points in one direction towards what has happened to others, in another direction to what I am.[7]

We are usually able to determine what motivated someone to act in a certain way, but because the consequences and responses to the action are part of the action, it is difficult to ascertain when or how an action ends. A narrative provides a solution for this in giving an action a certain *magnitude*, starting with its antecedent conditions and ending with its consequences, intended and unintended, including the responses it let to.

Both the action's consequences and the demands for a response may extend far beyond what was and could be envisioned by the actor the moment she acted. This also holds true for the actor herself, who, afterward, may regret the harm she did, intentionally or unintentionally, and demand from herself to make things right. The historian too is part of the chain of consequences, asking for a response when they describe an action and hence hold the actor accountable for her deed, even if the actor can no longer comply with the request. Here the point is that narrative exercises an *authority* over what has been done, and not just over what has intentionally been done.[8] This authority is especially pregnant in the case of history. Arthur Danto puts it thus:

> It is a commonplace piece of poetic wisdom that we do not see ourselves as others do, that our image of ourselves is often signally different from the image held by others, that men constantly over- or under-estimate the quality of their accomplishments, their failures, and their dispositions. ...These discrepancies are nowhere more marked than in history, where in the nature of the case we see a man's behaviour in the light of events future to his performances, and significant with respect to them.[9]

A narrative allows us to evaluate actions in terms of their wider bearings, which the agent did not and could not intent nor know, and they would have given a great deal for having this knowledge if they could, Danto adds. Knowing the intended and unintended consequences of actions, and their connection to later events, is the advantage that historians have over actors and their contemporaries: They have the privilege, as Danto calls it, of seeing actions in temporal perspective.[10]

The connection between action and narrative is a central concern of this Element. This connection is not incidental, albeit that actions can be understood without narrative. Some authors – including authors in the debate on history as a mode of knowing – argue for an even closer link between action and narration,

---

[7] Williams, *Shame*, 92. [8] Williams, *Shame*, 69. [9] Danto, *Narration*, 183.
[10] Danto, *Narration*, 183.

making the concepts mutually dependent. An action, they argue, is suggestive of a sequence that exhibits a narrative structure, with a beginning, middle, and end, where the actor, being caught in the middle, and given her character, pursues some end in response to the circumstance as perceived by her. One implication is that the events that historians study are already narrative in character, and hence, a further refinement of the actor's own understanding of what she did.[11] Alasdair MacIntyre puts it succinctly:

> It is because we understand our own lives in terms of the narratives that we live out that the form of narrative is appropriate for understanding the actions of others. Stories are lived before they are told – except in the case of fiction.[12]

MacIntyre would say that Odysseus *enacted* a narrative the moment he started his journey home – if he indeed was a historical person. Each of us is a character in their own drama, which provides the model for understanding others.[13] There is little that MacIntyre offers in support of his view. It is one thing to state that situating an action in a narrative makes the action intelligible, whether the action is our own deed of that of someone else, but it is quite another to state that narrative is *necessary* for understanding actions and ourselves, and therefore, that we live a story.

MacIntyre opposes Louis Mink in the passage we just quoted, who claimed that stories are not lived but told, since only "in retrospective stories are hopes unfulfilled, plans miscarried, battles decisive, and ideas seminal."[14] But, MacIntyre states, this is not the issue, as it holds true for the actor as well. Retrospective understanding is not only part of the way an actor understands herself and her doings after the deed, but it is also something she anticipates when she acts.[15] Hence stories are lived, even if one only is in part its author. But we should not agree with MacIntyre.

Note that the discrepancies between what an actor knows and can know, what her fellow actors know and can know, and what the narrator knows and *discloses* to the audience, bit by bit, are key features of narrativity, which exploit these discrepancies, whereas they are *not* features of our action. Telemachus did not know that Odysseus was alive, and Odysseus did not know what was going on at home, but the audience knows both these things. The audience also knows what both Odysseus and Telemachus did not, even though they at times

---

[11] Carr, *Time*, 46. [12] MacIntyre, *After Virtue*, 246. Carr, *Time,* 70, agrees with MacIntyre.
[13] MacIntyre, *After Virtue*, 248–249. Bewildering – and baseless – is his claim that "The unity of a human life is the unity of a narrative quest." MacIntyre, *After Virtue*, 253. Already Aristotle disagrees with this view in his *Poetics*, 51a16ff. Bernard Williams criticizes some of MacIntyre's views in his "Life as Narrative," 305–317.
[14] Mink, *Understanding*, 60. [15] MacIntyre, *After Virtue*, 250.

suspected it, which incidentally too is a feature of narrativity, that Athena was on their side, who acknowledged the injustice that was done to Odysseus, and guided them when needed. The audience knows about Odysseus's ruses, of which those who are affected by it are typically ignorant, and only the narrator knows beforehand whether Odysseus's plan will succeed or not. When I act, I may wait and see how things turn out and assess my action's success or failure. But I do not know at the time of the action what its consequences will in fact be.

This might not persuade MacIntyre and others. David Carr, who agrees with MacIntyre, for instance, after discussing the sort of discrepancies just mentioned, asserts that "we are constantly striving, with more or less success, to occupy the story-teller's position with respect to our own actions."[16] Not only in our personal life, but in our social life as well, in terms of the story we tell ourselves as communities:

> To tell the story of the community and of the events and actions that make up its history is simply to continue, at a somewhat more reflective and usually more retrospective level, the story-telling process through which the community constitutes itself and its actions. ..... For the *we*, no less than for the *I*, reflectively structuring time in narrative form is just *our* way of living in time.[17]

We not only take up the external narrator's position, next to the internal character's position, but narrative has a practical function in our lives as well, and "we sometimes assume, in a sense, the point of view of audience to whom the story is told, with regard to our own action."[18] Carr does not give an example of this latter claim, but think of Odysseus being incognito at the court of the Phaeacians, where the bard Demodokus sings about his war efforts and the pain and suffering he endured because of it. Here Odysseus is the audience of his own action, and he is moved to tears by the story. However, he would strongly disagree with the claim that his actions and sufferings *amount to* "a process of telling ourselves stories, listening to those stories, and acting them out or living them through." The retrospective view is not, as Carr concludes, "an extension and refinement of a viewpoint inherent in action itself."[19] The viewpoint from the narrator, and what she discloses to the audience, is already there at the very moment the actor acts, who has no say in what this viewpoint is like. And this is something that MacIntyre and Carr crucially missed: I cannot understand my action at the time of acting in terms of future consequences that have not yet obtained, whereas narrators can, which they may disclose to their audience to

---

[16] Carr, *Time*, 61. Peter Goldie makes the same point in his *The Mess Inside*, 26.
[17] Carr, *Time*, 177.   [18] Carr, *Time*, 61.   [19] Carr, *Time*, 61.

achieve the effects they aim at in term of the narrative's plot, both of which are at odds with the actor's viewpoint.

The sort of discrepancies I mentioned between what is known and disclosed, and the suspension they create – will the ruse work out as planned? – are essential to the progression of the tale. They are features of the plot that gets the audience involved and steers the sympathy the audience has for its characters. Something is precisely tragic or comical because the actor knows not what the audience knows, and when the actor finally finds out what the audience knew all along, there is a sense of relief, felt by both actor and audience. There are many other features of narrativity. Here the point is that the concepts of action and narrative are *not* mutually dependent. This is not to deny that narrative is a primary form of human (self)understanding, nor is it to deny that narrative is primarily concerned with action. Our interest here is in history as a discipline, and the historian's advantage of seeing actions and their consequences in temporal perspective. The discrepancy between what the actor knows and can know, and what the historian as narrator knows and can know, is an important reason why historians rely on narrative.

The narrative structure of beginning, middle, and end should not be associated with actions, as MacIntyre and others erroneously stipulate, but with what Aristotle refers to as the one complete action that each successful narrative represents. Aristotle praises Homer for adhering to this rule.[20] The one complete action, the vicissitudes it involves, and the resolve its ending brings, he calls the plot (*muthos*): the arrangement of the incidents. After the narrative's end, and before its beginning, nothing happens that affects the plot, which is the "soul" of the narrative.[21] The *Odyssey* starts with Odysseus being held captive by the nymph Kalypso, with the Gods discussing his fate, while Telemachus watches in dismay as Penelope's suitors squander their family fortune. It ends with Odysseus and Telemachus, and two of their loyal servants, killing the suitors to restore their house, after which Odysseus reunites with his wife and his father, bringing the resolve that is typical of narrative. The end of Odysseus's house being restored, and the justice of it, is already there at the beginning of the tale, and it is constantly anticipated as the story progresses, giving it the *unity* or "whole" (*holos*) we associate with narrative. This unity is what qualifies the work of historians as a narrative, or so this Element holds. It is the second central concern in this Element.

The *Poetics* is well known for distinguishing history from fiction, reducing the former to a chronicle of unrelated events. But in passing, while having the narrative in mind rather than the chronicle, Aristotle does conclude that epic

---

[20] Aristotle, *Poetics*, 51a22-29. [21] Aristotle, *Poetics*, 50a38, 50b23-50b33.

poets "make the structure like that of history."²² To be sure, this leaves the distinction between history as being concerned with what actually occurred and fiction as being concerned with what might have possibly occurred but did not, intact.

This Element's interest is in narrative as a mode of knowing. It draws attention to the epistemic value of historical narrative *qua* narrative. With historical narratives I have today's academic monographs in mind. It is important to note that historians also *comment* on the actions and sufferings they relate, the evidence they have, and the work of their fellow historians, stemming from their analysis, and as such, they do not narrate.²³ But these comments serve to support their *narrative thesis* – its message or point of it all – which could not be expressed otherwise. The emphasis on narrative therefore does not mean that historians are storytellers rather than critical reasoners.²⁴ Narrative, rather than "merely a literary device employed for arbitrary or traditional reasons," is "*a way of thinking*,"²⁵ a cognitive instrument, as Mink has it. Here the concept of narrative also includes the so-called cross-sectional histories that do not tell a story with a clear beginning, middle, and end. Instead of adopting a diachronic storyline and letting the events speak for themselves as elements of a story, these histories portray an age, offering an aerial or panoramic view of a period.²⁶ The claim that historians propose theses on the past I draw from the work of Frank Ankersmit.²⁷

As is often the case, while leaving the elaboration of his claims to others, Mink perceptively observes that:

> It is the narrative history *itself* which claims to be a contribution to knowledge, not something else which the narrative history merely popularizes or organizes. The claim of a narrative history is that its *structure* is a contribution to knowledge, not just a literary artifice for the presentation of a series of factual descriptions.²⁸

The structure that Mink mentions, on which he does not elaborate, is what Aristotle refers to as the *muthos* and the result of what we will call the narrative

---

[22] Aristotle, *Poetics*, 59a29. Paul Ricoeur therefore is right to start his analysis of history-writing with Aristotle's notion of plot. See his *Time*, 31–51, where he emphasizes the *synthesis* that the plot allows.

[23] When the poet speaks for herself, she does not represent, Aristotle, *Poetics*, 60a6, notes. Gallie, *Philosophy*, 66, writes: "every genuine work of history is also a work of reason, of judgment, of hypotheses, of explanation," next to being "a species of the genus Story."

[24] Jouni-Matti Kuukkanen uses this false opposition in his *Postnarrativist*, 67.

[25] Mink, *Understanding*, 176.

[26] Mink uses the term aerial, *Understanding*, 57. Frank Ankersmit uses the term panoramic instead, *Narrative Logic*.

[27] Ankersmit, *Narrative Logic*, 2.   [28] Mink, *Understanding*, 168.

thesis. The temporal whole or unity we associate with narrative, the one complete action that each narrative represents, with its beginning, middle, and end, stems from the thesis that historians propose. As such, the narrative thesis allows for an intelligibility that is peculiar to narratives.

Mink's contention that a narrative's structure is the historian's contribution to knowledge raises the questions what counts as the beginning and end of a historical narrative, what knowledge is specific to narrative, how it is justified, why historians rely on narrative, how narratives relate to one another, and how we choose among them. This Element aims to answer these questions.

1 Narrative's Indispensability

Historians often casually refer to their work as a narrative or a story. Narrative is a primary form of human understanding. It also is a way of thinking. But why do academic historians rely on it? To begin to answer this question, we best look closely at some historical monographs and search for features of narrativity. The books discussed will be with us throughout this Element.

1.1 Two Examples

In the opening chapter of his *Andean Cosmopolitans. Seeking Justice and Reward at the Spanish Royal Court*, José Carlos de la Puente Luna thus delineates the subject of his book in time and space:

> It centers on the journeys of indigenous subjects from the jurisdiction of the *Real Audiencia de Lima* (the Royal High Court of Appeals) – in one of the most important and largest cities within the viceroyalty of Peru – to the royal court of the Spanish Habsburgs and back to the Andes. It covers the period from the first expeditions of conquests into the Inca realm in the 1530s to the Habsburg Dynasty's twilight in the late 1690s.[29]

This passage mentions two sets of complex actions – the journeys and the expeditions – and it alludes to a third set of actions that have to do with litigation. As the subtitle of Puente Luna's book indicates, the Andean travelers were seeking justice and reward at the Spanish Royal court. There is clearly a story to tell, or numerous stories to tell, about these journeys, the viceroyalty of Peru, and the expeditions of conquests. But there is no reason to assume that a narrative structure is necessary to make the actions intelligible. We may perfectly understand the journeys to the Habsburg court and their purpose without reverting to narrative. The question is not whether historians can tell stories, for surely, they can, as most if not any other human being can. The

---

[29] Puente Luna, *Andean Cosmopolitans*, 5.

question is why narrative is indispensable for their work. The passage quoted does not provide an answer to this question.

Two terms however do point toward narrative, or at least toward the sort of temporal structure we associate with it: Here I am thinking of the terms "first" and "twilight." The former is a future-referring term, suggesting in this case that there were more expeditions to come, whereas the latter is a past-referring term, suggesting a past in which the Habsburg dynasty dawned and established itself.[30] These terms are in other words suggestive of a temporal whole, the one complete action (*muthos*) in Aristotle's sense that each narrative represents, which in this case appears to *begin* with the expeditions of conquests and *ends* with the twilight of the Habsburg dynasty. From this we may infer that Puente Luna's narrative, apparently, is concerned with a chapter in the life of the Habsburg dynasty. And even if he composes his work thematically, which he does, this dynasty's *career* figures as the narrative's backbone. Puente Luna, however, does not tell the story of conquest, the empire's growth and its twilight: He merely alludes to it in the passage we quoted. He studies the Habsburg rule from the perspective of the Andeans: "This story reconstructs the worlds of Andean travelers to the Habsburg court form the inside out."[31] Rather than being concerned with a chapter in the life of the Habsburg dynasty, his narrative is concerned with a formative chapter in the life of the Andeans. Interestingly, Puente Luna writes that his account is part of a larger story: He aims to inscribe the histories of Amerindians "in the larger narratives about the formation of the Atlantic world."[32] We will come back to this in Section 3, as it raises the important questions how historical narratives relate and whether they can be combined to form one single, comprehensive narrative. But first we try to pinpoint why histories require narrative.

A few lines later after the passage we quoted, Puente Luna writes:

> An unprecedented movement of peoples, goods, and ideas across the Atlantic marked the beginnings of the modern era. Overseas voyagers, in particular, *wove* the webs of early modern European empires. Andean, notably indigenous travelers to the Habsburg court, belonged to this world in flux.[33]

Again, the complex actions referred to are the overseas voyages. Note, however, that the voyages of Andean travelers to the Habsburg court, pleading their cases, are *redescribed* as weaving the web of early modern European empires, and the start of the voyages back and forth is redescribed as marking the beginnings of the modern era. Note also that the verbs used – weaving and marking – do not describe a complex action, albeit that they are redescriptions

---

[30] More on these in Section 2 of this Element. [31] Puente Luna, *Andean Cosmopolitans*, 15.
[32] Puente Luna, *Andean Cosmopolitans*, 6. [33] Puente Luna, *Andean Cosmopolitans*, 5.

of them: There are no such complex actions as weaving an early modern empire or beginning a modern era, as these are not things anyone can *do* in the same sense that one can travel, plead a case, plan an expedition, or conquer a kingdom. Now we begin to see why narrative is indispensable: They make a specific sort of redescription possible, in which actions are described in terms of their contributions to a development over time, which the narrative represents. With the overseas voyages, the modern era starts, which entails the creation of a series of connections – a web – that made the early modern European empire.

To know what Puente Luna means with these redescriptions, we need to read his whole narrative, and not only the passage we just quoted, for it is the narrative that makes these redescriptions possible and provides their substantiation. Each sentence the narrative contains contributes to its central message, Ankersmit holds, albeit that one sentence will be more important for identifying its message than the other:[34] "the reader of a work of history must always read each individual statement as the component of a much larger set – namely, of that work of history *as a whole*."[35] With the redescriptions that we singled out, Puente Luna *indicates* what the *thesis* or message of his monograph is. It is a gesture to his readers, helping them to grasp the message which the narrative as a whole substantiates. *His* idea of the emergent modern world is specific to his narrative. This is why narrative is indispensable. A narrative redescribes the actions and events it relates in terms of its thesis, which allows for its being a whole, a complete action in Aristotle's sense.

Someone might observe that in the passage I just quoted, Puente Luna identifies the modern era with globalization, albeit without using the term. Indeed, and Puente Luna is explicit about this identification when he writes that the Amerindians helped forge "the connections that gave the first century of the global age its defining character."[36] But if this is so, then why is the meaning of the emergent modern world, and hence of globalization, specific to his narrative, as I suggested? Is not globalization simply the world becoming interconnected? And does it not suffice to describe globalization as the movement of peoples, goods, and ideas? Why, then, is narrative indispensable to the historian? The point is that what globalization means in the context of Puente Luna's narrative is different from what it means in the context of, for instance, Timothy Brook's *Vermeer's Hat: The Seventeenth Century and the Dawn of the Global World*.[37] The difference is not obvious at first. Brook's work centers on paintings of Johannes Vermeer as "windows on the past" and opens with

---

[34] Ankersmit, *Narrative Logic*, 65.   [35] Ankersmit, *Representation*, 23.
[36] Puente Luna, *Andean Cosmopolitans*, 13.   [37] Brook, *Vermeer's Hat*.

a comparison of seventeenth-century Shanghai and Delft.[38] He too uses the term globalization in the sense of the movement of peoples, goods, and ideas, just like Puente Luna, albeit exchanging the Atlantic for the Indian ocean. So why, then, is Puente Luna's idea of the emergent modern world, which apparently comes down to globalization, specific to his narrative when the term can be properly defined and used across every narrative dealing with the movement of peoples, goods, and ideas, and the interconnected and interdependent world that results from it?

The use of the term globalization here is not to be limited to the issue of correctly applying this concept, albeit that both Brook and Puente Luna do correctly apply the term when they use it. This is what we expect not only from historians but also from any capable language user. But that is not what is of interest here. The terms they use – the beginning of the modern era, the dawn of the global world – rather are shorthand *names* of the narrative thesis they propose. Not distinguishing between these two uses causes a great deal of confusion.[39] One easily sees the distinction when one realizes the following. It is not that historians would say: Puente Luna is right, globalization started in the sixteenth century, and Brook is wrong to claim that the seventeenth century was the dawn of the globalized world, as the subtitle of his book has it. Nor would any trained historian say: Puente Luna omitted to discuss Vermeer's painting and Brook failed to incorporate Andean travelers to the Spanish Royal court. One can put forward a definition of globalization, of modernity, of early modern empire, and use that to describe phenomena. Historians, like any other language user, apply concepts and they must do so correctly if they are to qualify as competent language users. But Andean travelers cocreating the early modern empire is a *narrative thesis* that gives the phenomena associated with globalization in the narrative its specific meaning, by redescribing these phenomena in terms of it. This is why the term "globalization" acquires an *autonomy* in Puente Luna's book vis-à-vis "globalization" in Brook's book.

We do not read Puente Luna's monograph to discover that the modern era begins with the expeditions and conquests in the Inca realm. That is not its cognitive message. We also do not point at histories that locate the beginning of the modern era elsewhere and search for evidence to find out who got the facts straight, as the beginning of the modern era depends on a narrative rather than on some fact of the matter. We also do not read Puente Luna's book to discover that globalization is the movement of goods, peoples, and ideas across oceans: We may consult a dictionary for that. We read Puente Luna's narrative because

---

[38] The book starts with a personal anecdote of Brook in his twenties cycling southwest from Amsterdam, finding shelter and hospitality in Delft.

[39] van den Akker, *The Exemplifying Past*, 114–117.

we are interested in the making of the Atlantic world, and in the role of Andeans and their elites, and how they adapted to the new sociopolitical reality enforced upon them. The journeys undertaken to seek justice and reward are charged with "social and political significance," Puente Luna writes.[40] This underlies that history as a discipline is concerned with the field of action and the practical knowledge associated with, and more specifically with the social and political context of it.[41] The historian's task is to discern the historical significance of these actions, and after she has successfully done so, the past is made intelligible to us. With Puente Luna's narrative at hand, we look at the Andean travelers to the Habsburg court and see how the early modern Habsburg empire is co-constructed by their efforts and how new forms of indigenous leadership emerge under their rule in Peru.[42] Such is its cognitive value. As has been often remarked, *all* histories are concerned with societal *change*, with a world in flux, as Puente Luna calls it. To be sure, historians may be interested in why something remained the same, but without change, there is no history, and hence no need for historical narrative.

Identifying the thesis with the cognitive message of a historical narrative makes evident why historians need narrative, and how it is different from other types of texts. The message afforded by narratives cannot be reduced to the sentences it contains. If that would be so, a narrative's content could be expressed without it, and no narrative thesis would be required. Obviously, we can state the thesis of each narrative apart from it, but to know what the thesis means requires reading the whole narrative, which is precisely meant to substantiate the thesis. So much must be clear. A historical narrative is not merely the story of actions in temporal perspective. Each action the historian relates connects to the overall message she wants to communicate. Seeking justice and reward is what the Andean travelers to the Spanish Royal court did, but the cognitive value of Puente Luna's narrative is found in how these travelers from the sixteenth century onward cocreated the early modern Habsburg empire. That is the one complete action, in Aristotle's sense, that Puente Luna's narrative represents.[43] This one complete action is not something

---

[40] Puente Luna, *Andean Cosmopolitans*, 6.
[41] Hayden White observes: "Hegel was right when he opined that genuinely historical account had to display not only a certain form, namely, the narrative, but also a certain content, namely, a politicosocial order." White, *The Content of the Form*, 11.
[42] Puente Luna, *Andean Cosmopolitans*, 17.
[43] The term representation has been scrutinized by philosophers of history. See Eugen Zeleňák, "Two Versions of a Constructivist View of Historical Work," 209–225; and Zeleňák, "Representation," 299–315. The sense there is different from Aristotle's sense of the *muthos* being a *mimesis* (representation) of one complete action.

Knowledge and Narrative

that is part of the course of events, but rather that which gives us a grasp of it, allowing for its unity.

The Andeans becoming part of the Habsburg empire in the Andean world is what ends or concludes Puente Luna's narrative, providing the actions it relates with the unity we associate with narrative. It is not something anyone intentionally did or planned, even though it resulted from their actions. A term such as "the early modern Habsburg empire" at first glance seems to refer to a large-scale event, but on closer inspection it refers to the specific conception proposed by Puente Luna of the incidents related. A narrative, we said in the preface following Aristotle, represents one complete action, one temporal whole with a beginning, a middle, and an end. The one complete action that each narrative represents we refer to as the narrative's thesis. The thesis that the Andean travelers co-constructed the early modern Habsburg empire determines the narrative's beginning. The establishment of the empire is the ending to which the actions and events related are oriented toward from its beginning, creating the unity typical of narrative. A narrative thesis is the cognitive messages that historians convey, and which they *see-in* the events they study and relate.[44] It qualifies the work of historians as a narrative.

Let us consider another historical monograph: Glenda Sluga's, *The Invention of International Order. Remaking Europe after Napoleon*. This is the second book that will be with us in this Element. Both Puente Luna's and Sluga's narratives are exemplary pieces of historical scholarship and representative of the field. I just happen to have come across them because of personal interest. Since the use of narrative is indispensable, they should qualify as such. Note that the sophistication of these works tends to get lost in the use I make of them here.

The thesis of Sluga's book is as follows: "In this book, the end of the Napoleonic wars is the origin of the modern international order."[45] This order, as the title indicates, is *invented*. It coming into being in the aftermath of the Napoleonic wars is the societal change that this monograph is concerned with. The allusion to narrative is immediately there: One chapter in the life of the international order ends, another begins, and the same event is described both as an end *and* a beginning. The diplomatic efforts of heads of states, their foreign ministers, and non-state actors such as Germaine de Staël can each be assessed in terms of their intended and unintended consequences, and in terms of the ethos underlying them, but the central message that Sluga's narrative offers is

---

[44] For the term, see Van den Akker, *Exemplifying Past*, 13, 107, 112, 119–120, 124–125, and 145.
[45] Sluga, *International Order*, 9.

concerned with the *invention* of the modern international order in post-Napoleonic Europe. Here's one of the key events she discusses:

> One of the most unprepossessing symbolic moments in the history of European diplomacy takes place around a small cardplaying table in the "dirty and dull" northern French town of Chaumont, on the river Marne. On 9 March 1814, at the Coalition's makeshift headquarters, the foreign ministers of Russia, Prussia, Britain, and Austria take a vow to pursue their alliance into the postwar period.[46]

The event referred to is a diplomatic meeting, but a specific one, and its importance lies in the act of foreign ministers vowing to pursue their alliance. The vowing is an entity that can be assigned a specific location in space and time, allowing us to individuate this event.[47] The same goes for the events Sluga connects this event with, such as the Coalition's war against Bonaparte and France, "very dull" meetings at Chatillon, and the signing of the treaty at Chaumont. The granularity with which the event is described, and the details added, is up to the historian. Note that the events here are actions. All actions are events, but not all events are actions. An event is something done or something that happens to someone, at a specific location in space and time.[48] By describing the meeting of foreign ministers on March 9, 1814, at a small cardplaying table in Chaumont as a symbolic moment in the history of diplomacy, Sluga points at the historical significance of the event. What this significance is remains undisclosed in the passage. But we already know the thesis that Sluga proposes: The modern international order is invented in post-Napoleonic Europe. The meeting in Chaumont is one of the events exemplifying this thesis.

Sluga ends her introduction thus:

> By asking, "What kind of ordering was embedded in the invention of the politics that could take place between states two hundred years ago?" we stand to learn more about the practices and assumptions that still temper the international order today, for better and for worse.

This is the sort of *practical* wisdom one finds in her narrative, and which derives from the thesis she proposes:

> Ultimately, my attention to invention reveals how international politics came to bear the imprint of the political culture of the modern liberal state, with its bourgeois gender and class norms, and its concurrently inclusive and exclusive universal, imperial and European, national and international foundations.[49]

---

[46] Sluga, *International Order*, 87.   [47] Davidson, *Actions and Events*, 209–210.
[48] This suffices for our purpose here. There is of course much more to say about events. See Assis, *Plural Pasts* and Assis, "Shapes and Functions of Historical Events."
[49] Sluga, *International Order*, 10.

History is concerned with the field of action and the practical knowledge that is associated with it.

1.2 Narrative and Events

Descriptions featuring verbs individuating an event usually refer to some project the actor is involved in, such as the pursuance of an alliance, waging a war, or seeking justice and reward. One may suppose that such descriptions can be *standardized*, similarly to the sort of standardized description that theory and analytical categories allow. This may be considered a mark of disciplinarity, or science even. Think of standardized descriptions about the working of diplomacy, forming alliances, continuing wars, and litigation, but these, and the sort of description we are considering here, do not help us to understand the cognitive value of narratives. Mink points out that this is not because standard descriptions are impossible to arrive at or because they are undesirable – they are not:

> It is rather because if it were successful it would render narrative form wholly superfluous for the understanding of events; for in stipulating standard descriptions of events (combined with the body of theory that such descriptions are designed to serve) it would rule out the redescriptions that are required in the construction of narrative.[50]

An action and the suffering it causes does not require a narrative to be intelligible, but at the same time the available stock of action-descriptions does not suffice in the eye of the historian. Sluga describes the action of vowing to pursue their alliance as a symbolic moment, as part of the history of European diplomacy, and, from the point of view of the narrative, as key to the postwar invention of the international order. These are the sort of redescription that are offered in narratives and why historians need them. In the case of Puente Luna's monograph, we too saw the need for redescriptions that depend on the narrative. We therefore should agree with Mink when he concludes that:

> "Events" (or more precisely, descriptions of events) are not the raw material out of which narratives are constructed; rather an event is an abstraction from a narrative. An event may take five seconds or five months, but in either case whether it is one event or many depends not on a definition of "event" but on a particular narrative construction which generates the event's appropriate description.[51]

Remember the meeting of foreign ministers in Chaumont on March 9, 1814. Its length can be calculated, if the evidence allows it, and the vowing to pursue the

---

[50] Mink, *Understanding*, 200.   [51] Mink, *Understanding*, 201.

alliance will take up a few seconds. But its appropriate description relies on their significance as a symbolic moment in the history of diplomacy. Narrative allows for the redescription of events in terms of it. Appealing to an event therefore usually comes with their significance already implied, that is, in terms of a narrative in which the event features.

Connecting later events to earlier events, and revealing their historical significance, is the historian's task. The sequence of events in a narrative unfolds as the events point toward some future resolution, such as the establishment of early modern Empire or the modern international order. The unfolding of events is grasped not by following their chronological order, but by this *promise* of resolution. The order of events is fixed and cannot be undone, but we do not understand the sequence of events in their chronological order. As Mink has it:

> To comprehend temporal succession means to think of it in both directions at once, and then time is no longer the river which bears us along but the river in aerial view, upstream and downstream seen in a single survey.[52]

Historians are no chroniclers, listing what happens the moment it happens in their chronological order.[53] Historians need not present the events they relate in a temporal sequence, as if their main task would be to tell a story. Usually, historians present their work thematically or cross-sectionally. In such cases, the events do not unfold before the eye of the reader, but their significance is presented instantly. The emphasis on the narrative thesis as that which qualifies the work of the historian as a narrative avoids the unfortunate identification of narrative with storylines. The main point here is that to ask for the historical significance of an event, as Danto and Mink hold, requires a narrative in response. Danto:

> To ask for the significance of an event, in the *historical* sense of the term, is to ask a question which can be answered only in the context of a *story*. The identical event will have a different significance in accordance with the story in which it is located or, in other words, in accordance with what different sets of *later* events it may be connected.[54]

In this passage, Danto talks about the identical event in different stories, whereas Mink in the earlier quote talks about events as abstraction from narrative. There is no contradiction here. Identity of events referred does not

---

[52] Mink, *Understanding*, 57.
[53] On the distinction between narrative and chronicle, see White, who associates the end of narrative with closure and the demand for moral meaning. White, *Content of the Form* 21–24.
[54] Danto, *Narration*, 11. See also Mink, *Understanding*, 47, 202.

entail identity of event-description. Two (different) event descriptions refer to the same event if the event referred to happens to have occurred at the same time and location. The point that both Danto and Mink make is that narrative allows for a redescription of events in terms of the *significance* it endows events with, thus generating the "the event's appropriate description." As Mink aptly puts it: "the description of events is a function of particular narrative structures."[55]

When historians appeal to past events, they do so in terms of their significance, that is, in terms of the sort of conceptions we associate with the narrative in which they might feature. It is up to the historian to decide on the significance of actions and events relative to her interests and the sort of questions these interests lead to. And what is once considered to be insignificant may turn out to be decisive at another moment.[56] There is an inexpungable subjective factor here – Danto even talks of "an element of sheer arbitrariness,"[57] but this subjective factor is firmly held in check by the field and the discipline that constitutes it. The discipline demands not only using appropriate methods of analysis but it also demands that a historical narrative is consistent with other narratives. How to understand this requirement of external consistency and how it connects to the evaluation of narratives will be discussed in Section 3.

In this introductory section, we centered on determining the historical significance of events for which narrative is indispensable. What follows focusses on seeing actions in temporal perspective, typical of narrative, and on the central message it conveys in terms of its thesis. Section 2 is concerned with the first, and Section 3 with the second.

2 Narrative Sentences

Events stand in a specific temporal relation to one another: Their order is fixed, and they are either past or future regarding one another, earlier or later. These temporal positions determine the sort of thing that one can say about them. Take the utterance that Danto's *Analytical Philosophy of History* is a classic. He would call the term "classic" a past-referring predicate "whose correct application to a present object or event, logically involves a reference to some earlier object or event which may or may not be causally related to the object to which the term is applied."[58] Calling Danto's *Analytical Philosophy of History* a classic now, in 2025, involves reference to the earlier publication date of the book in 1965. It would not have made sense to call the book a classic in 1965, or shortly afterward, let alone before 1965 when the book was not even published.

---

[55] Mink, *Understanding*, 201.
[56] This insight is key to the modern conception of history, as it came into being at the end of the eighteenth century. See Koselleck, *Futures Past*, 128–151. For the insight, see p.139.
[57] Danto, *Narration*, 142.   [58] Danto, *Narration*, 71.

The book only *acquires* the property of being a classic over time, and its reedition in 1985 is evidence of its status. Being a classic is just like patina and wrinkles a mark of pastness, and hence, evidence of existence in time. Being conscious of this existence in time, which books and bronze statues cannot, is to exist historically and "to perceive the events one lives through as part of a story later to be told."[59]

If someone called the book an *instant* classic in 1965, she would have expressed her enthusiasm about the work, underlining its importance to the field or referring to its positive reception in the year in which it was published. But the evidence for it being a classic in 1985 is different from the evidence for it being an instant classic in 1965. There was plausibly some evidence to predict in 1965 that the book would become a classic, but it is not the same evidence used to support the claim that the book is a classic in 1985. Historical inquiry is typically concerned with the latter relation between evidence and the claims it makes, whereas the former is typically used when forecasting the weather, an earthquake, or rising temperatures. The evidence these events will leave behind – their traces, if they occur – will be different from the evidence used to predict them. Typically, the relationship between statements about the past and the evidence supporting it is abductive in the sense given to it by Peirce.[60] "Footprints exist after, not before the event they testify to, and it is with such things that historiography has to do," Danto notes.[61] There is a difference between *predicting* (a future-referring term) that the book will become a classic and *having correctly predicted* (a past-referring term) this, as the latter requires *knowing* that the book *is* a classic, whereas the former does not. When someone states that Danto's book becoming a classic has been correctly predicted, reference is made to the earlier event of making the prediction, and this earlier event is redescribed in terms of the later event of the book having become a classic. This is the sort of sentence that Danto calls a *narrative sentence*.[62] The nature of these sentences is central to this section, as is their distinction from action-sentences that describe the sort of complex action we associate with projects and the good and harm they may have caused.

---

[59] Danto, *Narration*, 343.   [60] Danto, *Narration*, 122.   [61] Danto, *Narration*, 174.

[62] Danto is interested in temporal relations, and the time these relations refer to is their place on the timeline that keeps track of the Earth revolving around the Sun. Time is the number of movement, as Aristotle had it. This physical time is often distinguished from the phenomenal time we experience and have access to through introspection. It is relevant to point at this, as phenomenal time has, according to such authors as David Carr (mostly following Husserl) and Paul Ricoeur (mostly following Augustine and Heidegger), an inchoative narrative structure. We may grant Carr and Ricoeur their point, but it would not affect the sort of considerations pondered here. Cf. the Preface to this Element.

2.1 Tense and Narrative Sentences

Danto provides an extensive discussion of a class of statements the truth-value of which depends on the moment of its utterance.[63] Such statements are usually tensed sentences, and they not only assert something about the events they refer to but also inform us about the temporal position of the speaker. There are other temporal indicators used in this class of statements that typically are situational, most notably the attributes of past, present, and future, and there are differences between natural languages for doing so.[64] This is how A. J. Ayer, whose essay on statements about the past informs several of Danto's considerations, formulates it:

> The use of the present tense indicates, without necessarily stating, that the event to which the statement refers is contemporary with its formulation: the use of the past tense indicates that it is earlier, and the use of the future tense indicates that it is later. Tensed verbs are situational in the sense that they reveal the speaker's temporal standpoint relatively to the events that they are used to describe: and the same is true of the attributes of past, present, and future when they are used in conjunction with the non-temporal copula.[65]

As to the remark after the colon: Think of statements stating that a war is past, present, or future. Calling a war a future war *now* implies that it is future relative to the speaker's temporal standpoint, whereas calling it a past or a present war now implies that the war is past or present relative to the speaker's temporal standpoint. So much is clear. The important point that Ayer draws from it is that no statement as such is about the past, since "it is only from the point of view of someone who happens himself to occupy a later position that any statement comes to be about the past."[66] The same applies to statements about the present and the future. The phrase "past event" is thus a mere shorthand for "event in my past," or "event prior to my temporal position." Danto agrees: "being past is not a property of events, but a relationship in which events may stand as one term."[67] Events are not past, present, or future, but rather stand in a specific temporal relation to speakers. From a semantic point of view, we better think of "past," "present," and "future" as modal notions.

Not all statements are tensed statements. The truth-value of tenseless statements – or more precisely, the truth-value of the propositions expressed by such statements – do not depend upon the time of uttering them. Think of statements

---

[63] Truth-values are central to semantics since, as Davidson puts it, "a truth value is the simplest and clearest mark of the unity of sentences and of the beliefs and judgments that sentences can be used to express." Davidson, *Truth*, 120.
[64] For a more general discussion, see Dyke, "Time and Tense," 328–343.
[65] Ayer, *Philosophical Essays*, 184.   [66] Ayer, *Philosophical Essays*, 189.
[67] Danto, *Narration*, 54.

such as the Earth is a globe, copper melts at 1,085°C, and the Earth revolves around the Sun. The truth of these tenseless statements does not depend on the moment of their utterance. Putting such tenseless statements in a past or future tense therefore usually makes no sense. It would be odd for someone to say that the Earth will be or was a globe,[68] that at some point in the future copper will melt at 1,085°C, or that after Copernicus the Earth started to revolve around the Sun rather than the other way around. To be sure, the belief that the Earth revolves around the Sun is temporally indexed in that it depends upon a believer, but the truth-value of the tenseless statement is not. Our interest here is in the class of statements the truth-value of which depends on the moment of its utterance, that is, we are interested in statements containing temporal indicators. Verbs in their different tenses are such temporal indicators.

Tenses are means to indicate a temporal relation between what an utterance expresses and the moment of uttering the statement. Consider the following statements in their different tenses:

1.1. The war begins/began/will begin.
1.2. Jones is/was/will be planting a rose.

Or, to use historiographical examples drawn from Sluga:[69]

1.1. Peacemaking begins/began/will begin.
1.2. Foreign misters vow/vowed/will vow to pursue their alliance.

To determine the truth-values of these statements, we need to know the ordinary or lexical meaning of the words used and the grammatical rules followed. I will take the meaning of a sentence to consist of its truth-conditions: Understanding a sentence is grasping how to take the sentence – the way the words are used – on the occasion on which it is made. Note that in ordinary communication, the context makes clear what event and person is referred to. The following should be clear. In their present tense, the time of the event referred to and the moment of its utterance coincide. In their past tense, the time of the event referred to comes before the time of the utterance. In their future tense the possible (future) event referred to is to take place after the utterance of the statement. Tensed sentences inform us both about some object or event referred to and the temporal position of a speaker, which is why their truth-value depend on the moment of its utterance. If I utter the statement "Foreign ministers vow to pursue their alliance," then its truth-value depends on whether they indeed do take such a vow at that very moment. The statement is true when they are, and

---

[68] At least before or after our solar system acquired its current shape.
[69] Sluga, *International Order*, respectively, p.109 and p.87.

false when they are not. As for the future tense sentence, its truth-value is, for the time being, undetermined, as it cannot be known beforehand whether the future event will in fact obtain. But we *know* that this future tense statement too has a truth-value, albeit that we do not presently know what that truth-value *is*. The meaning of a sentence is given by its truth-conditions.[70] Future tense statements too have a meaning, and hence truth-conditions that need to obtain for the sentence to be true. We know that the foreign ministers will be gathering and perhaps we hope that they vow to pursue their alliance, but only after they in fact made their pledge, the truth-value of the future tense statement will be known.

Now consider a second class of statements, taken from Danto, each again in their different tenses.

2.1. The Thirty Years War begins/began/will begin.
2.2. Jones is/was/will be planting a prize-winning rose.

Or take the historiographical examples drawn from Sluga:[71]

2.1. The Concert of Europe begins/began/will begin as informal conversations.
2.2. Foreign ministers of the coalition forces lay/laid/will lay the conceptual planks on which the modern international order is built.

To determine the truth-values of these statements, we need to consider the time of the events referred to and the time of the utterances of these statements. There is no difference in this regard between the statements of class 1 and 2 in their past and future tenses. In their past tense, the time of the event referred to comes before the time of the utterance. In their future tense, the future event referred to is to take place after the utterance. So, at first glance, it does not seem to be the case that we are having two different classes of statements here. However, in their present tense – and this is different from what we see in the statements of class 1 – the time of the event referred to and the moment of its utterance do *not* coincide. This is remarkable. Why is that? First, we should note that in the case of statements of class 2, there is not *one* event referred to, but *two*: respectively, the beginning and the end of the war; the planting of a rose and the winning of a rose competition; the informal conversations and the resulting Concert of Europe; and the laying of conceptual planks and the resulting international order. Second, we should note that the description of the first event referred to requires the second event to have occurred, for only in 1648 did it make sense to claim that in 1618 a Thirty Years War began, and only after having won a prize

---

[70] This is central to Davidson. See for instance Davidson, *Truth*, 123.
[71] Sluga, *International Order*, respectively, p.89 and p.88.

is it true to talk about planting a prize-winning rose. The following is crucial: Although these statements are *linguistically* presented in the present tense, they are *semantically* statements in the past tense. Danto does not make this distinction, which explains a certain shortcoming in the discussion of some of the statements he ponders, as we will find out.

To determine the truth-value of statements of class 2, both events must have occurred. Danto calls this class of statements *narrative sentences,* and they are usually formulated in a past tense.

> Their most general characteristic is that they refer to at least two time-separated events though they only *describe* (are only *about*) the earliest event to which they refer. Commonly they take the past tense, and indeed it would be odd ... for them to take any other tense.[72]

The narrative sentence "The Thirty Years War began in 1618" refers to the beginning and end of the war but describes its beginning in 1618. Similarly, the sentence "Jones was planting a prize-winning rose" describes the planting in terms of winning the competition. Of the two events referred to, one event is future to the other, although both are past to the speaker. Terms such as "anticipates," "began," "gave rise to," and "correctly predicted" indicate that the sentence is a narrative sentence.[73]

It might seem odd to utter or read "The Thirty Years War begins in 1618" and even more odd if someone utters "The Thirty Years War will begin in 1618," but if we are able to distinguish between the linguistics and semantics concerned here, these sentences, odd as they may seem, do not pose any problem of correct interpretation. What is linguistically put in a present or future tense may semantically be a past tense statement. Such is typically the case with statements of class 2.

Typically, narrative sentences are a class of statements under which an event cannot be witnessed. Danto: "many, and perhaps the most important kinds of sentences which occur in historical writings give descriptions of events under which those events could not have been witnessed."[74] There is thus a specific limit to eyewitness reports. This is not a limit of historical knowledge, but rather a condition of it. Even the Ideal Witness – or the Ideal Chronicler as Danto also calls her – being able to describe an event as it happens the way it happens, including what goes on in the minds of those involved, is not able to describe the event she witnesses in terms of narrative sentences.[75] In 1618, no one could

---

[72] Danto, *Narration*, 143.   [73] Danto, *Narration*, 157.   [74] Danto, *Narration*, 61.
[75] Danto, *Narration*, 151. The term "ideal witness" has the benefit of specifying what is meant by an event as recorded by the Ideal Chronicler. This does not oblige us to accept any empiricist idea about observational knowledge: It merely accepts the existence of witness accounts. Cf. Mink, who observed that we can imagine an Ideal Chronicler because of the unwarranted

witness the start of the Thirty Years War since it was unknown how long the war would last. Similarly, no one could witness that Jones was planting a prize-winning rose, as it was unknown who would win the contest. And no one could ascertain that the aftermath of the Napoleonic wars the international order was invented. What the Ideal Chronicler chronicles in Danto's thought-experiment are possible observations a possible witness might have made, rather than fixed events, as their description depends on the sort of descriptions witnesses might have offered. Take the following example. The British foreign secretary Castlereagh remarked after the meeting in Chaumont that it signaled "a great moral change coming in Europe, and that the principles of freedom are in full operation." Sluga notes:

> From Castlereagh's view, Chaumont is the next logical step in an evolving politics. From our perspective, it gives a quasi-legal form and adds pragmatic detail to the accentuated multilateralism of the early nineteenth century, anticipating its international dimensions.[76]

Narrative sentences describe an event in terms unavailable to the historical persons involved or those witnessing the event.[77] This feature of historical knowledge does not contradict Quentin Skinner's famous maxim that "no agent can be said to have meant or achieved something which they could never be brought to accept as a correct description of what they had meant or achieved."[78] We should accept this maxim and it does not affect the logic of the narrative sentences discussed here and what it reveals about the structure of historical consciousness. Danto nowhere denies that historians describe actions in terms of action-sentences that reflect the agent's understanding of what she is about in the circumstance she is in.[79] This includes the antecedent conditions of actions and how they make the action intelligible. And this entails both attending to terms with which the actor understood herself and terms with which we

---

presupposition that "everything that has happened belongs to a single and determinate realm of unchanging actuality," a totality of "what really happened." Rejecting that presupposition turns the Ideal Chronicler into an incoherent notion. Mink, *Understanding*, 194–195. Paul A. Roth agrees with Mink, see his *Structure*, 28–29. Mink and Roth have a point, but they make too much of it. Danto just thinks of the Ideal Chronicler in terms of an ideal witness producing (ideal) observation reports, which is innocent.

[76] Sluga, *International Order*, 89–90.
[77] Mink notes that redescription of events may not only depend on knowledge of later events but also on new techniques of acquiring knowledge (think of techniques for identifying disease or economic conjunctures) and on new conceptual modes of analysis (think of Marxist interpretation of Roman proletariat). Mink, *Understanding*, 140–141.
[78] Skinner, "Meaning and Understanding," 77.
[79] This for instance is Frederick A. Olafson's complaint in his misreading of Danto. Olafson, "Narrative History and the Concept of Action," 265–289, there 276. This misreading is found elsewhere in the literature too. See for instance Ahlskog and D'Oro, "Beyond Narrativism," 5–33.

understand it. His example throughout his book concerned the Thirty Years War. We understand the actions of the Palatine Elector, Frederick, with reference to his ambitions. Think of his efforts

> to gain ... and regain the crown of Bohemia. His various negotiations with France and England, his attempts to raise money and to secure alliances. Yet his actions had, at every turn, consequences which he never intended and which, in view of our ignorance about the future, he *could* not have intended. Yet it is in view of these consequences, and in terms of their wider bearing upon the Thirty Years War, that his actions have acquired, in historical perspective, the significance they have.[80]

By describing an earlier event in terms of a latter event, thus creating a specific temporal relation and continuum between events, a minimal sense of narrative is suggested. This is not to say that narratives are defined by the narrative sentences they happen to contain. According to Danto, narrative sentences "are frequently used to justify the *mention*, in a narrative, of some thing or event whose significance might otherwise escape a reader."[81] Such sentence may present the significance of the period under consideration in one single statement. This is what, for instance, Sluga does in the preface to her book: "The intention of this book is to return to the early nineteenth century as the origin of the conception of international order that shaped modern international politics."[82]

2.2 Project-Verbs

One specific form of temporal relation that Danto draws our attention to is what he calls *project-verbs*. Think for instance of the sort of projects the Palatine Elector was engaged in, such as trying to regain the crown of Bohemia; or of the project of the Andean travelers Puente Luna studies so closely, who sought justice and reward at the Habsburg royal court; or think of the efforts of Germaine de Staël, building a coalition against France. These project-verbs – trying to regain the crown, seeking justice and reward, building a coalition – will deepen our understanding of the distinction between the two classes of statements we have been discussing, although statements of class 2 are distinctive of them and point toward their (narrative) structure. Let us return to the first class of statements.

1.1. The war begins/began/will begin.
1.2. Jones is/was/will be planting a rose.

Or a historiographical example of it:

---
[80] Danto, *Narration*, 182–83. [81] Danto, *Narration*, 167. [82] Sluga, *International Order*, xi.

1.1. Peacemaking begins/began/will begin.
1.2. Foreign misters vow/vowed/will vow to pursue their alliance.

We can distinguish these statements thus: The 1.1. statements are event-sentences, whereas the 1.2. statements are action-sentences. For something to be an action it must be intentional under one of its descriptions, even though other (non)-intentional descriptions may exist, which is usually the case. For something to be an event it must have been brought about or happen to someone or something. The distinction between action-sentences and event-sentences is rudimentary but suffices for our purpose here. Nothing hangs on it. I want to single out action-sentences wherein someone is doing something, and which assumes there to be a description under which the deed is intentional. Such descriptions have a more or less prominent place in historical narratives, depending on the interests of the historian and how she sees the role of human agency in history, which may vary significantly. Danto is interested in the verb, the doing, and calls the predicate "is R-ing" a project-verb.[83] Think of the examples we started with: trying to regain the crown, seeking justice and reward, and vowing to pursue an alliance.

We might think that, in contrast to what we have been saying, the sentences 1.2., in all three different tenses, refer to two time-separated events, namely, the planting and the rose coming about. In the present tense, Jones is planting a rose at $t-1$, and at $t-2$ we indeed observe that it is a rose that was planted. In the past tense, Jones started planting a rose at $t-1$ and at $t-2$ he indeed can be said to have planted it, given the coming about of the rose. In the future sense we gather that Jones intends to plant a rose at $t-1$ and that this intention includes the rose coming about at $t-2$. In each tense, it seems, an earlier event (planting a rose) is, *covertly*, described in terms of a later occurrence (the rose coming about). If project-verbs covertly describe an action in terms of a later occurrence, as we are suggesting here, then they are covert narrative sentences, and the distinction we made between the two classes of statements falls apart. This conclusion is however too hastily drawn, since the distinction remains intact, and it is revealing to see how this is so.

If Jones is planting a rose, or repairing a radio, and when the coalition forces are vowing to pursue their alliance, it may well be that the rose will not come forth, the radio may not be repaired, and the alliance may fall apart before it is established. So, in a sense, reference is made to a future event (the rose being planted, the radio being repaired, the alliance being in effect), but this future event need not come about for the sentence to be true.[84] This is different with narrative sentences. For a narrative sentence to be true, both events referred to

---

[83] Danto, *Narration*, 161.   [84] Danto, *Narration*, 164–165.

need to have occurred. So, sentences with project-verbs are *not* (covert) narrative sentences.

Project-verbs do point to a temporal structure. But the sentences they appear in are logically different from narrative sentences. Consider the following statements:

2.2. Jones is/was/will be planting a prize-winning rose.
2.2. Foreign misters of the coalition forces lay/laid/will lay the conceptual planks on which the modern international order is built.

Planting is a project-verb. The verb "planting" in this narrative sentence is however not, since although one can try or hope to plant a prize-winning rose, one cannot do it. Perhaps someone objects and argues that this is true in the present and future tenses, but not in the past tense, since, if Jones won a prize for his rose, he did in fact plant a prize-winning rose when he was planting a rose. In response, we should first keep in mind the distinction between linguistics and semantics, as statements of class 2 can linguistically be put in different tenses while semantically remaining statements in a past tense: Narrative sentences cannot semantically be but past tense statements. Our objector momentarily forgot this. Second, Jones only was planting a prize-winning rose after he won the prize. The narrative sentence requires the future event (winning the prize) to have come about for the sentence to be true, and this is not the case for sentences with project-verbs. The temporal relations that project-verbs point to are different from the temporal relations typical of narrative sentences. Tenses are not of relevance here. Sentences such as "Jones is/will be/was planting a rose" or "Jones is/will be/was repairing a radio" do not logically imply that the actor succeeds in what he is, will be, or was doing.

Since the Ideal Witness is capable of describing what people are doing the moment they are doing it, we should endow her with the ability to use project-verbs. But she cannot make use of narrative sentences, as such sentences require foreknowledge of the future which the Ideal Witness has not. The historian has the advantage of knowing what later events can be connected with earlier events, and this advantage "the actor, and his own contemporaries, could not in principle have had." Historians, Danto writes, "have the unique privilege of seeing actions in temporal perspective."[85] One last observation. The verbs used in such phrases as *starting* the Thirty Years War, *planting* a prize-winning rose, *inventing* the international order, and *weaving* the web of early modern empire are semantically *not* project-verbs, even though they linguistically appear to be ones; rather they point toward narrative sentences that describe an earlier

---

[85] Danto, *Narration*, 183.

occurrence in terms of a later one, and as such they already point toward narrative. We may think of verbs in phrases of statements 2.2. such as "planting a prize-winning rose" or "laying the conceptual planks for the modern international order" as concepts that summarize a *scenario* in terms of resolutions or endings.[86] This is what a narrative sentence using these verbs captures. Narrative sentences are, in Paul Ricoeur's apt phrase, "a plot in miniature."[87]

2.3 Truth-Value Link

In chapter 4 of his book, Danto offers an extensive analysis of Ayer's views of verifying statements about the past. One of the problems Ayer was concerned with, in Danto's reading, is how we can have knowledge of the past if there is nothing for us to observe. This is a classical problem in the philosophy of history if there is one: Our empirical knowledge is knowledge of what there is, and hence of something which is not past but present. It is rather elementary to accept the view that statements about the past are true if they can be verified, that is, confirmed by the evidence and the methods of studying it. Here it matters whether we have a representational or inferential understanding of confirmation. Nothing hangs on it here. Verification is a sufficient and not a necessary condition of empirical statements being true.

One response to the problem would be to point out that our knowledge of the past is inferred from its remains: its traces, including memories, and these we observe and study in the present. So, statements about the past are in fact statements justified by the best evidence we have for them in the present. Ayer and Danto are not satisfied with this answer. Their concern is semantical rather than epistemological. The remains from the past as evidence allow us to talk about what our knowledge of the past is based on. It does not, Danto notes, provide us with a way to talk about the past.[88] The point is that we should not equate statements about the past with statement about present evidence. Such equation makes the past intrinsically inaccessible and that betrays a misunderstanding of how we use tenses. A second response to our problem too is to be dismissed, notably the response that statements about the past are covert predictions of future observations. Such prediction of future observation as part of historical inquiry makes sense – think of predicting what one will find while excavating some archaeological site or when browsing through a newly discovered box with notes of lectures by Hegel. But again, this concerns talk

---

[86] I do not think that a story's emotional structure is a better expression of the sort of scenarios captured by summary concepts, as David Velleman apparently thinks, and for which one looks in vain for evidence in his essay. See Velleman, "Narrative Explanation," 1–25, at 19.
[87] Ricoeur, *Time*, 148.   [88] Danto, *Narration*, 44.

about what our knowledge of the past is based on rather than talk about the past itself.

How, then, to talk about the past without equating it with talk about present or future observations? To answer this question, we need to remember that statements about the past inform us about the temporal position of the speaker regarding the object or event referred to. Second, we need the concept of *truth-value link*. Take once more the statements of class 1.

1.1. The war begins/began/will begin.
1.2. Jones is/was/will be planting a rose.

In its present tense, we may say that the statement is true when an eyewitness is present to witness the start of the war or the planting of the rose. Her observation verifies the statement and as long as we have no reason to doubt her testimony, we may accept the statement to be verified and hold it to be true. This is a mere basic feature of being a language user (if we would remove this basic feature, we would not be able to understand what it means to possess a language, since someone possessing a language then would be incapable of communicating what can be instantly pointed at). We may add that the statement, once uttered, keeps its truth-value when time passes. This we refer to as the truth-value link.[89] If at $t-1$ I or someone else observes that the war begins or Jones is planting a rose, we accept at $t-2$ that at $t-1$ the war began and Jones planted a rose. The past tense thus is connected – linked – to the present tense of the statement and presupposes it, thus keeping its truth-value. Note that this is not the case for statements of class 2, which is obvious as there is semantically no present tense of the statement to begin with. There was, at $t-1$, nothing to observe or infer, nothing to experience that would verify the statements of class 2. Note also that for our class 1 statements, the truth-value link concerns one direction only: A past tense statement is linked to a present tense statement and presupposes it. Finally, note that there is no truth-value link between the present and future tenses of the statements. Predicting at $t-1$ that some event or situation will obtain at $t-2$ does not mean that at $t-2$, the event or situation referred to at $t-1$ came about.

The truth-value link between a statement in its present and past tenses raises the following question: How do we know that the truth-value link exists? Answering this question gives us a third response to the problem we started with: How to talk about the past without equating this talk with talking about present evidence? This response is offered in terms of Ayer's notion of "verifiable in principle," which Danto discusses and Michael Dummett more recently

---

[89] Dummett, *Enigmas*, 363.

rediscovered.[90] The verifiable-in-principle principle states that if I, or anyone else, happen to be at the start of the war or the planting, I, or anyone else, would in principle be able to observe the starting or infer it from something else. The statement therefore *could have been* verified.[91] That is part of what the statement *means*. Note that the verifiable-in-principle principle makes use of the truth-value link. If I, or anyone else, state that this or that is so-and-so at $t-1$, it is true, at $t-2$, that this or that was so-and-so at $t-1$. Understanding the statement in its past tense at $t-2$ involves knowing that at $t-1$ the statement could have been verified. Note also that we separate the question what a statement says and means from what is needed to verify the statement, that is, to establish that it is true.[92] The truth-values of statements of class 1 made in the past tense are not limited to what counts as evidence for them in the present. This was our objective: We want to discuss our talk about the past rather than our talk about present evidence. And this we achieved for statements of class 1.

What about the statements of class 2? Semantically, they are statements in a past tense, and therefore, there is no truth-value link between a present and past tense. But there is more to it. A narrative sentence redescribes an earlier event in terms of a later event, hence the events these sentences refer to need to have occurred, and hence be past to the speaker.[93] This entails that, in principle, both events could have been verified, albeit not under the description given by the narrative sentence before the second event has occurred. So, implicitly, the truth-value link is there in that the events referred to must have been verifiable at the time of their occurrence, albeit not under the description offered by the narrative sentence.[94] This points toward narrative and the discrepancy between the sort of description given by actors and those of the omniscient narrator. Jones cannot plant a prize-winning rose if he did not plant a rose. The Thirty

---

[90] Danto, *Narration*, 46ff.

[91] Dummett, *Truth and the Past*, 44–45, 64–65. See also already Dummett, *Enigmas*, 368. Cf. Williams, "Another Time, Another Place, Another Person," 164–173.

[92] Dummett, *Truth and the Past*, 50–52. Conflating this distinction leads to anti-realism. The notion of a truth-value link moves us away from anti-realism about the past. There is a tendency to assert that the statement about the past is true given the evidence available and the methods of studying it. But the verifiable-in-principle and the truth-value link it makes use of opposes this view and claims that a statement about the past is true if the statement in principle could have been made, even if there was no one there to make it. The conclusion is that statements about the past are not statements about present evidence.

[93] Compare the following. Only those events we can reasonably predict to happen in the future, given the knowledge we have, that can be said to be once future, then present, and then past. The end of the Thirty Years War in 1648 was never in the future (although some sort of end was). The end of the war only became future to the beginning of the war after 1648.

[94] This agrees with Ahlskog's claims that "(i) agent-centred perspective is internal to the very idea of historical knowledge, and (ii) that the agent-centred perspective is epistemically prior to retrospective (re)description." Ahlskog, "Pre-narrativist Philosophy of History," 195–218, at 195. It does not conflict with narrativist philosophy of history, as Ahlskog suggests.

Years War cannot last thirty years if the war did not start. And the international order cannot be invented if there was no context in which representatives of states acted. As the historian Glenda Sluga puts it: "With the advantage of hindsight, the international, even cosmopolitan, aspects of this early nineteenth-century multilateralism are defined by what we know international thinking will become."[95] Narrative sentences do not erase possible contemporaneous observations of the event they are about and redescribe in terms of a later event the sentence connects it with. An event is something brought about or endured, and hence must be known under some description by the actors involved before it is redescribed at a moment later in time.

2.4 Truth

Let us return one last time to our first class of statements.

1.1. The war begins/began/will begin.
1.2. Jones is/was/will be planting a rose.

These statements are true in their present and past tense when the events referred to take place or have taken place and false when they do not. This agrees with Aristotle, who is praised by Danto for taking time seriously, and his claim that "whatever is present or past is unambiguous in the required sense, namely, that sentences about these are definitely either true or false."[96] Danto questions this claim in the context of narrative sentences and compound sentences part of which is a narrative sentence: "sentences whose truth or falsity is contingent upon the truth or falsity of some sentence about the future," as Danto – misleadingly, as we will see – puts it.[97] Let us accept Aristotle's definition of truth: to say what is that it is not, or of what is not that it is, is false, while to say of what is that it is, or of what is not that it is not, is true. And let us take true sentences to be sentences that correspond to clearly individuated facts.[98] Consider once again the narrative sentences:

2.1. The Thirty Years War begins/began/will begin.
2.2. Jones is/was/will be planting a prize-winning rose.

---

[95] Sluga, *International Order*, 88. [96] Danto, *Narration*, 191.
[97] Danto, *Narration*, 194–195. Danto, *Narration*, 192, also observes the following problem: "suppose we speak of the beauty of Napoleon's fifty-seventh wife. There was no such woman. Yet a statement about her would be a statement about the past and must be definitely true or false, if Aristotle is right." It is a statement about the past inasmuch as is concerned with Napoleon, but then the statement is false since he has no fifty-seventh wife. It is not a statement about the past inasmuch as it is concerned with "Napoleon's fifty-seventh wife," as there is no such person in the past. There is therefore no such problem.
[98] This is of course not to be confused with the idea that true sentences are true or false because of "the way things are." Davidson, *Truth*, 126.

Danto suggests that in their present tense, these sentences are neither true nor false: Their truth and falsity depend on whether the events referred to obtain in the future, and hence, on what can be said about them in the future. So contrary to Aristotle's claim, there are statements about what is present that are neither true nor false. This is misleading if not simply erroneous, for as we have been emphasizing throughout this section, even though statements of class 2 may linguistically be put in a present tense, they are semantically past tense statements and cannot be otherwise. So, Aristotle's claim, *pace* Danto, still holds. But now consider compound sentences, part of which is a narrative sentence. Take the following example from Danto.

> Talleyrand begat Delacroix and Delacroix will paint the *Mort de Sardanapale*.

Is this sentence true? If it is, Danto reasons, then the sentence

> Delacroix will paint the *Mort de Sardanapale*

is true as well, whereas the sentence is not according to Aristotle, as only statements about what is either past or present are definitely either true or false.[99] But Danto is mistaken. Although this narrative sentence is linguistically put in a future sense, it semantically is a past tense statement, and hence agreeing with Aristotle's claim that statements about the past and present are definitely either true or false. So there is no reason to question Aristotle's claim in the context of a compound sentence, part of which is a narrative sentence.

The point that Danto wants to make is that the sentence

> Talleyrand begat the man who painted the *Mort de Sardanapale*

is true at one time, whereas it is false or neither true nor false at another.[100] So far so good. If we distinguish between linguistics and semantics, these sentences do not pose any problem of correct interpretation. We know that the truth of the sentence depends on the existence of both the man and the painting. All narrative sentences – and all compound sentences containing a narrative sentence – are semantically past tense sentences and therefore are in a definite sense true or false. The issue to Danto is that there is a certain *past-contingency* at stake in the sense that an earlier event can be redescribed in terms of a later event, but what later event is used for such description is dependent, for one, on its future contingent occurrence *and* the future contingent interests of the historian, both of which are unknown to contemporaries of the event. This we agree with. For as long as the future is open, these past

---

[99] Danto, *Narration*, 195–196.   [100] Danto, *Narration*, 196.

contingencies exist, and hence no complete description of past events can be given.[101] Any account of the past is essentially *incomplete*.[102]

Every time someone utters a statement about the past or present, the statement is in a definite sense either true or false. To be sure, a person can be mistaken and can *take* an utterance to be true which is false and vice versa, and which she may learn about. The point is that an utterance has truth-conditions that either obtain or not in the circumstance the utterer is in, and the utterance will not be understood if it is unclear under what conditions it would be true.[103] As for statements about the past and present being either definitely true or false, there seems to be one crucial exception, and this concerns those statements in a narrative that state its thesis. Such statements are often narrative sentences, which, we said, too are in a definite sense true or false, but they cannot be identified with them. This is one of the issues we turn to in the next section. A few remarks are in order.

Take our examples: the invention of the international order and the co-construction of early modern European empire. Are these statements of the respective narrative theses in a definite sense true or false? Since they are statements about the past, they presumably are. This, however, is not the case. What is crucial to note here is that the meaning of the statement of a thesis depends on the respective narratives that uniquely substantiate it. *Accepting* the statement of a thesis therefore implies accepting (all) the statements in the narrative that elaborate on them, thus accepting the narrative as a whole as the thesis's embodiment.[104] Although statements about the past in a narrative are in a definite sense true or false and substantiate its thesis, the statement of the thesis itself is neither true nor false. Narratives define the circumstance to assent to statements about the past. This explains why a statement of a thesis is neither true nor false, since it is not something one assents to; rather, it provides the context for assenting to the statements the narrative consists of. Thus, the statements in the narrative justify the thesis it proposes.

3 Narrative Theses

The previous section was concerned with narrative sentences and sentences featuring project-verbs and their distinction. Here our concern is with narratives as semantic vehicles in their own right, irreducible to the statements they are made of. A narrative redescribes the actions and events it is about in terms of the thesis it *expresses*. Hence, the actions and events that the narrative references

---

[101] Danto, *Narration*, 197. [102] Danto, *Narration*, 16–17.
[103] Davidson, *Truth*, 50, 123, 141.
[104] This is the central claim of Ankersmit, of both his *Narrative Logic* and his *Representation*.

exemplify the thesis.[105] Expression and exemplification are the semantic values appropriate to narratives. A *statement* of a narrative thesis is a *synoptic judgment* which allows us to see things together in a single act of understanding, as Mink puts it. This statement resembles a command, which also is neither true nor false, commanding us: see the past in these terms!

3.1 Stating the Thesis

We start by turning to the two examples we are already familiar with:

1. Andean travelers are seeking justice and reward at the Spanish Royal court.
2. The modern international order was invented in post-Napoleonic Europe.

The first sentence is an action-sentence in which "seeking" is the project-verb. The second sentence is not an action-sentence, although it appears to be one. The distinction is important. Action-sentences that describe complex actions, the sort of which we associate with projects, usually suggest that there is a story to tell, given the rights or wrongs they caused, but the actions they refer to need not be situated in a narrative sequence to be intelligible. We perfectly understand the first sentence on its own, and any further elaboration of it does not necessarily require narrative. Now look at the second sentence. This too appears to be an action-sentence in which "inventing" features as the project-verb. But since no one could intentionally invent the modern international order and the shape it actually acquired over time, it cannot be one. Therefore, calling the invention a project and the sentence an action-sentence is misleading.

Someone may object to this and point out that for something to be an action, it must be intentional under one of its descriptions, and there are many actions that the second sentence redescribes as inventing the international order: the vowing to pursue the alliance at Chaumont, the efforts of Staël, and so on. So no harm is done by calling it an action-sentence, our objector concludes. But the point is to distinguish between (1) action-sentences and (2) statements of a narrative thesis. The latter are indeed redescriptions of actions, but redescriptions that depend on narrative: They require a narrative both for its intelligibility and its justification. This dependency is easily recognized. Sluga redescribes the actions of diplomats and non-state actors in post-Napoleonic Europe in terms of her narrative thesis that their actions constitute "the origin of the conception of international order that shaped modern international politics."[106] To understand the thesis, we need to

---

[105] Exemplification is reference running back from denotatum – the actions and events – to symbol – the narrative thesis. Goodman, *Language of Art*, 65. For its adoption in the philosophy of history, see Van den Akker, *The Exemplifying Past*.
[106] Sluga, *International Order*, xi.

read her entire narrative, which is the justification for it. The thesis qualifies the work as a narrative. This too is not difficult to recognize. The invented modern international order is the narrative's *end* or *conclusion*, to which all the actions and events it describes are orientated toward. We need not be surprised that this conclusion is already presented at the start of her book, as this is typical of all narrative endings: They *must* be there in the beginning to guide the reader along.

The distinction between action-sentences and statements of narrative theses overlaps with that between action-sentences and narrative sentences. Often the statement of a narrative thesis is a narrative sentence, but they should not be identified with one another. A narrative sentence is intelligible on its own, but the statement of a narrative thesis requires the narrative to substantiate it. To further grasp the distinction, let us look at the example we quoted earlier, this time from Puente Luna's book:

> An unprecedented movement of peoples, goods, and ideas across the Atlantic marked the beginnings of the modern era. Overseas voyagers, in particular, *wove* the webs of early modern European empires.[107]

These two sentences are, in isolation, both narrative sentences, though one is inclined to take the first sentence to be intelligible on its own and have some reservation whether this holds for the second sentence. Marking the beginning and weaving the webs are not project-verbs in action-sentences. In the passage, Puente Luna *redescribes* the movement of peoples, goods, and ideas across the Atlantic in terms of the later and large-scale event of the modern era coming about, and he redescribes the overseas voyages in terms of the later and large-scale event of the coming about of early modern European empires. Note that both sentences state, albeit in different words, Puente Luna's narrative thesis: Andean travelers co-constructed the early modern Habsburg empire. For a proper understanding of the two sentences, this connection to the thesis is vital, as it provides the proper context for the sentences: We need to understand the two sentences in terms of the narrative thesis.

The statement of a narrative thesis usually takes the form of a narrative sentence, and usually they are scattered throughout the text. In the narrative they function as reminders to the audience of the central message or point that they should get out of it. Throughout his book, Puente Luna at times, but not frequently, refers to the temporal whole that his thesis is concerned with, using terms such as "early modern," "in the aftermath" or "since the time of conquest," and "the Habsburg era." He, however, mostly focusses on thick

---
[107] Puente Luna, *Andean Cosmopolitans*, 5.

Knowledge and Narrative 35

descriptions of indigenous travelers and their journeys, taking their historical significance as tacitly known to the reader – he did, after all, make their significance explicit in the opening chapter of his book. But every time the reader asks: Why should I know this? Or: Why is this of historical interest?; they are reminded of how what they read substantiates the idea that the early modern Habsburg empire is co-constructed by these travelers and their search for justice and reward. Take the following example from its third chapter:

> The activities of local, regional, and transatlantic Andean travelers and petitioners that this chapter follows were particularly influenced by the imperial system of justice that Andeans coconstructed in the second half of the sixteenth-century.[108]

The latter alludes to the beginning of the modern era referred to above, and it implies the sort of temporal perspective on actions typical of the historian's narrative. The idea of co-construction suggests a project, but not the sort of which can be described in standard action-sentences, as it requires a narrative: Co-construction is not a project-verb. A few lines later, Puente Luna remarks the following on the Andean travelers:

> Strong interpersonal links – ties of kinship, clientage, and authority, along with traditional habits of deference – were as important for them in their efforts to cross the Atlantic as they were for other early modern individuals and communities.[109]

Here Puente Luna implicitly connects his work to the larger narratives of the early modern Atlantic world, which he explicitly does in the opening chapter of his book. Here the connection is merely mentioned rather than elaborated upon. This is how historians work, and part of the mystery of their discipline: It points toward the requirement that a historical narrative is consistent with other narratives, in a sense to be spelled out below. It raises the important questions how narratives relate, how they are evaluated, and whether they can be combined to form a single and larger narrative. These questions will concern us in this section.

Where Puente Luna references his thesis sporadically and implicitly, albeit its being constantly there, underlying everything he states, Sluga does so rather frequently and more explicitly. She constantly reminds the reader of how the modern international order is invented in the aftermath of the Napoleonic wars. Take the following example of Sluga ending a section.

---

[108] Puente Luna, *Andean Cosmopolitans*, 54.   [109] Puente Luna, *Andean Cosmopolitans*, 54.

> [I]n combination with her own actions and her salon, Staël's ideas of liberty and independence were integral to the making of war and peace, and a new international politics.[110]

This is directly followed by the start of a new section.

> Germaine de Staël's life is an unavoidable axis for this history of diplomacy, in which the past is represented by a cosmopolitan brotherhood and the uncomfortable accommodation of the agency of women, and the future by the rise of national diplomats and a masculine bureaucratic diplomacy.[111]

Here Staël's life is the focal point of the history of diplomacy, from which both its past and its future are seen. Sluga makes full use of narrative as a way of thinking here, its temporal unfolding and the aerial view it allows. The significance of Staël's actions, including the responses to it, are key to the invention of the modern international order: They exemplify it. To know what Sluga means with it, we need to read the entire narrative, and everything she mentions in it exemplifies this invention. Such is typical of narrative: A narrative represents one complete action, as Aristotle taught, with a beginning, middle, and end. Sluga represents the one complete action of inventing the international order, beginning in the aftermath of the Napoleonic wars, and ending in its being established in what she loosely refers to as the modern era. The end or conclusion is a resolve, bringing occurrences in line in terms of what they led up to. Note that this end is not the fulfillment of some destiny inherent in the historical process: Historians deeply worry about such teleology, and they are experts in contingency and the idiosyncratic dynamics of each singular situation; rather, the end is the significance that historians discern in the events they study, which is captured by their narrative thesis.

Both Puente Luna's and Sluga's works are model works of history, and one is not better than the other simply for including more reminders of its unifying message. At most, one could conclude that Sluga pays more attention to getting her narrative thesis across than Puente Luna does, helping the reader along as she closely studies her book. Both these monographs make clear that narrative theses, or conclusions as Mink calls them, are *ingredient to* the narrative rather than *detachable from* it.[112] The thesis they propose enables the unity of the work. That is what a thesis is for, and what qualifies the work of historians as narratives.

A thesis is the narrative's central message. Mink refers to the statement of a narrative thesis as a *synoptic judgement*, which he describes as "seeing-things-together" in a "single act of understanding," whereas the narrative as

---

[110] Sluga, *International Order*, 24.   [111] Sluga, *International Order*, 24.
[112] Mink, *Understanding*, 79.

embodiment of the thesis is what we may refer to as an *interpretative synthesis*.[113] Mink identifies the two, but we need to distinguish them. A thesis, as a judgment in the Kantian sense of the term, points toward the faculty of understanding and the synthesis it allows. But a statement of a thesis cannot be taken as a substitute for the narrative as a whole. We do not stop reading Sluga when we read that the early nineteenth century is the origin of the international order. What she means by that thesis requires reading the whole narrative. Here I follow Ankersmit and his claim that all sentences in a narrative are to be understood in terms of the narrative thesis they together embody.[114] He uses the term "narrative substance" for what Mink refers to as the interpretive synthesis. In his most recent work, Ankersmit refers to the statement of the thesis as a meta-sentence tying individual sentences together.[115] A meta-sentence is about the narrative and about its sentences. The statement that the modern international order is invented in post-Napoleonic Europe is about Sluga's narrative and about its sentences, as each sentence explicates what this invented order is.

All of this is rather abstract. The two historiographical examples will help throughout this section to grasp the nature of narrative theses. In what follows, I will argue that the statement of the narrative thesis – the synoptic judgment – is something for which the historian is responsible: She must be able to provide *reasons* for it when she is asked for it. Since the narrative embodies the thesis, the narrative as a whole is precisely meant to provide this justification. Sluga's thesis that the international order was invented in post-Napoleonic Europe is justified by everything she says in her narrative. Similarly, Puente Luna's thesis that Andean travelers co-constructed early modern empire is justified by his narrative, and nothing short of it.

For a proper understanding of the nature of these narrative theses, we need to realize the following. The theses that historians propose, and for which narrative is indispensable, have no basis in fact, that is, they are not empirical theses that can be tested to confirm or disconfirm them. This does not involve a skeptical stance toward historical knowledge. Not at all. Rather, a thesis is *seen-in* the past remains and the past actions and events that can be inferred from them. Put differently, a narrative thesis does not reflect but is reflected in the actions and

---

[113] Mink, *Understanding*, 82. Mink is close to Gallie here, who writes that historians insist on "the 'interconnectedness of events', and on the need of synoptic mastery of a period or epoch if one is to contribute genuinely to the interpretation of even a minor corner or facet of it." Gallie, *Philosophy*, 53.

[114] According to Ankersmit, statements in a narrative have a double function. They assert something about the past and they define the thesis of the narrative. Ankersmit, *Narrative Logic*, 104. Ankersmit, *Representation*, 17.

[115] Ankersmit, *Representation*, 20.

events it is concerned with. It makes the past intelligible to *us*: that is what they are for. Since the epistemic adequacy of a narrative thesis does not depend on the evidence or what can be inferred from it, we need to rethink their epistemic status. It would be a mistake to limit the epistemic evaluation of narratives to the use of evidence in support of the singular statements it makes about the past, and forego the epistemic evaluation of narratives qua narratives, or deny the latter's relevance all together. This Element's title is precisely meant to draw attention to the epistemic value of historical narrative *qua* narrative.

If a thesis cannot be more or less accurate in the empiricist sense of the term, if there are no empirical grounds for preferring one thesis above the other, how, then, are theses accepted, logically compared, and on what grounds do we prefer one thesis above the other? Mink admits that he left these crucial questions open.[116] A first clue to answer these questions is by reference to the criteria of what a proper thesis amounts to: It needs to be comprehensive and allowing for consistency, and, as Ankersmit argues, it needs to have a maximum *scope*. These criteria allow us to discuss theses and prefer one thesis over the other. In what follows, I will argue that a narrative needs to be *externally* consistent by being consistent with other and rival narratives. Without the requirement of external consistency, no comparison nor preference would be possible. We already know that the narrative thesis allows for the narrative's *internal* consistency, its unity, as it redescribes the actions and events it relates in terms of it. How to conceive of external consistency is still to be determined.

A narrative thesis needs to be connected to rival theses, which they are meant to improve upon, thus contributing to historical knowledge and intervening in the debate about the topic it is concerned with. Sluga, for example, notes shortcomings in other works, but also a recent and renewed attention to the post-Napoleonic era. Puente Luna, as we already saw in Section 1, aims to inscribe the history he narrates "in the larger narratives about the formation of the Atlantic world."[117] This in turn suggests that narratives aggregate, which, since narratives have a unity of their own, they cannot. We will address this dilemma at the end of this section.

3.2 Ingredient Conclusions

In the debate about narrative as a mode of knowing, authors emphasize the distinctive conclusion that narratives afford. Narratives are not a special kind of *argument*, and the conclusion they offer is very different from it, as it does not follow from a set premises, nor is it derived from the evidence studied by the

---

[116] Mink, *Understanding*, 88.   [117] Puente Luna, *Andean Cosmopolitans*, 6.

historian. Walter Gallie was the first to point this out.[118] Mink further elaborated on it. A conclusion of an argument can be detached from its premises, and that, Mink observes, is not the case with the conclusion of a narrative, which are ingredient to it. On these *nondetachable* conclusions he writes:

> an historian is apt to "summarize his conclusions," thus giving the impression that the latter, like the detachable conclusion of science, are inferred from the evidence, rather than being indicators which point to the way in which the evidence has been ordered.[119]

Ankersmit agrees with Mink and observes:

> The ending of a narration is not a kind of shorthand of what was told before; nor is it possible to reconstruct a number of premises that would lead up to the ending of the narration in the way this can be done in an argument.[120]

The term "conclusion" can be somewhat misleading. Not only because of its association with detachable conclusions but also because it suggests that it comes at the end of the reasoning process. The conclusion or thesis, as I prefer to call it, is *seen-in* the evidence and what can be inferred from it, and as such, starts rather than ends the reasoning process, with the narrative being the result of this process. This, again, shows that the narrative thesis or conclusion qualifies as the ending of a narrative, and the resolve it brings, as Aristotle would have it, which guides our interest from the start: "it is chiefly in terms of the conclusion – eagerly awaited as we read forward and accepted at the story's end – that we feel and appreciate the unity of a story," Gallie writes.[121]

Argument and thesis are not always easily distinguished. Take the following example. The imperial judicial system developed gradually. Puente Luna concludes:

> The most significant historical development was the production, accumulation, and transmission of the legal capital that came to sustain a series of eighteenth-century campaigns orchestrated by the Indian elite of Lima and their rural allies.[122]

---

[118] Gallie, *Philosophy*, 24, 28–29. For the distinction between argument and thesis, with historiographical examples, see Van den Akker, *The Modern Idea of History and Its Value*, 122–127. For another recent discussion of narrative conclusions, see Imaz-Sheinbaum, *Historical Narratives*, 32–34.

[119] Mink, *Understanding*, 83. Mink's distinction between ingredient and detachable conclusions is anticipated by Gallie, *Philosophy*, 24, who distinguishes between the conclusion following from premises and a story's conclusion.

[120] Ankersmit, *Narrative Logic*, 47. See also Ankersmit, *Representation*, 200.

[121] Gallie, *Philosophy*, 29. Ricoeur agrees with Gallie and this connection to Aristotle's *Poetics*. See his *Time*, 150–151. Cf. White, who associates the end of narrative with closure and the demand for moral meaning. White, "Narrativity," 21–24.

[122] Puente Luna, *Andean Cosmopolitans*, 55.

The judicial system being developed from the second half of the sixteenth century onward in response to Andean travelers seeking justice and reward is an empirical claim that needs proof by evidence. The system has long-term effects, not only into the eighteenth century as the quote states but also into the twentieth century, Puente Luna notes elsewhere in his book.[123] The system as it developed and its long-term effects are empirical phenomena, and the conclusion that they have long-term effects can be inferred from the evidence. Understanding these long-term effects requires a temporal perspective unavailable for those involved, but it can do without narrative. So where does the need for a narrative thesis arise, then?

To distinguish argument and thesis we need to ask about the historical significance of the phenomena under consideration. It is the latter which requires the thesis, and the temporal perspective associated with it, which underlies and unites the empirical claims the historian makes, thus making those claims dependent on the thesis. Take another example. One can argue, as did Brian Vick, that women-led salons in post-Napoleonic Europe were sites of influence-politics.[124] The plausibility of this claim depends on the evidence for it. It is an empirical claim that can be confirmed or disconfirmed. But the historical significance of these salons for the invention of the international order cannot be inferred from the evidence, and therefore it cannot be confirmed or disconfirmed: It requires a narrative for its substantiation. As Mink has it: "The logic of confirmation is appropriate to the testing of detachable conclusions, but its ingredient meanings require a theory of judgment."[125] This theory of judgment is what this section is concerned with.

By distinguishing ingredient conclusion typical of narrative from detachable conclusions typical of argument and, we may add, science, we underline the specific cognitive value of narrative and its pattern of justification. The narrative *is* the justification of the theses that historians propose. An ingredient conclusion, as Paul Roth following Mink puts it, "cannot be supported or elucidated independently of the narrative that exhibits it. The narrative constitutes, in this specific sense, its own unique pattern of justificatory argument."[126] Note that "argument" is used here in the sense agreeing with Mink's ingredient, nondetachable conclusions, and not with the detachable conclusions that are ordinarily associated with arguments.

---

[123] Puente Luna, *Andean Cosmopolitans*, 18–19.   [124] Sluga, *International Order*, 5.
[125] Mink, *Understanding*, 84.
[126] Roth, *Structure*, 93. See also Ankersmit, *Representation*, 199–201. See also Kuukkanen, *Postnarrativist*, 94. Sometimes he, mistakenly, appears to hold that historians argue for a thesis and provide evidence for it (e.g., 79–80, 91), as if a thesis is a detachable conclusion.

A historian does not reference evidence or past events to demonstrate or prove the truth of the thesis she proposes. Rather, the historian references the thesis to explicate why the evidence and the past it is a witness of are what they are, and not otherwise. This we may call the principle of sufficient reason, which requires a careful interpretation. This principle does not, for instance, concern the reasons Sluga gives for why Staël organized salons the way she did or why she tried to build a coalition against France; it concerns the reason why those salons are of historical significance, that is, why they were instrumental in the invention of the modern international order.[127]

3.3 Narrative Explanation

The narrative as justification of the thesis it proposes is further strengthened in terms of the specific *explanation* that narratives afford. This concern with narrative explanation is central to the debate about narrative as a mode of knowing.[128] Sluga does not ask what caused the invention of the modern international order. Puente Luna does not ask what caused the emergence of early modern empire. To know what early modern empire and modern international order are, we need to read their respective books. Rather than asking for causes, they make clear what they mean with these terms. The supposed events to be explained – the emergence and the invention – and its explanation, are the result of their work rather than their starting point. Roth puts it thus:

> narratives explain only by virtue of the narrative order itself. . . . the events to be explained, and the events used to explain it, turn out to be part and parcel of the narrative to which they belong. A narrative constructs both the explanans and the explanandum.[129]

So Sluga does explain the invention of the international order, but what needs explaining (the *explanandum*) – the invention – is created by the narrative itself (the *explanans*). Sluga's whole book is concerned with precisely that. Puente Luna explains the emergent, early modern European empire and globalizing world. But this emergence – the explanandum – again is created by his very narrative, which itself provides the explanans for it. When the historian wonders

---

[127] I might add that there are events that are without sufficient reason in this specific sense, and in this sense alone, and which thus *defy* being redescribed in terms of some narrative thesis, even though they can – and should – be included in the narrative. These are events that defy any abstraction, such as the slaughter at Verdun.

[128] For a criticism of earlier and less convincing views, see Dray, "On the Nature and Role of Narrative in History," 25–39.

[129] Roth, *Structure*, 14. Roth expands on it, see especially *Structure*, 20–21 and 65–81. See also Gallie, *Philosophy*, 124, who concludes: "historical explanations cannot be directly supported by 'hard' historical evidence, since the question about any historical explanation is not a question of fact, but of the best way of arranging facts."

what caused the early modern European empire or the international order to come into being, they do not go looking for causal relations, but they devise a narrative embodying a thesis about the past.[130] This does not deny that the efforts of head of states, diplomats, and non-state actors in post-Napoleonic Europe causally affected the relations between states and the way diplomacy was conducted. The emergent international order in the early nineteenth century, shaping modern international politics, indeed was the result of numerous initiatives, ideas, beliefs, and interactions. But it is not something someone set out to bring about after the Napoleonic wars, as Sluga casually remarks in her epilogue.[131] The point is that seeing their efforts as inventing the international order for the centuries to come, requires (a) the perspective of the historian who sees those actions in temporal perspective unavailable to the actors involved, and (b) a thesis structuring those actions and their resolve in the one complete action of inventing the international order. Similarly, Andean travelers did not willingly and knowingly cocreate the Habsburg empire and the way it took shape over time. The point is not that Spanish conquests did not have consequences, such as Andeans traveling to its court. There obviously is this causal connection. But no conquistador, no Andean traveler, not even Charles V himself, intentionally brought about the early modern Habsburg empire, even though Charles V and his successors, with their apparatus, actively worked on building that empire. The co-construction of early modern European empire requires a thesis that structures and redescribes the actions in terms of it.

The (statement of the) Sluga's thesis that the international order was invented in post-Napoleonic Europe and that of Puente Luna that Andean travelers cocreated early modern empires cannot be detached from their books. To understand what they mean with them, we need to read their books. They are ingredient conclusions that are *exhibited* rather than *demonstrated*, exemplified rather than empirically justified by the available evidence.[132] Since conclusions (theses) are ingredient to their narratives, historians do not and cannot adopt one another's conclusions, and hence, their narratives do *not aggregate*. This raises the question we already posed before: How, then, do narratives relate? Mink formulates this question in the form of a dilemma, which he does not resolve: "narrative histories should be aggregative, insofar as they are histories, but cannot be, insofar as they are narratives."[133] At the end of this section we will be able to resolve this dilemma.

---

[130] Ankersmit, *Narrative Logic*, 237.   [131] Sluga, *International Order*, 269.
[132] Mink, *Understanding*, 79. See also Van den Akker, *Exemplifying Past,* 109–112.
[133] Mink, *Understanding*, 197.

3.4 Contributing to Knowledge

Sluga and Puente Luna are explicit in addressing how their work relate to that of their fellow historians. Sluga's Introduction and Puente Luna's first chapter are for the most part concerned with this. This is a methodological principle and a common practice among historians,[134] and usually they are trained to start their work with a *status quaestionis* regarding the subject they are writing about. After having made clear what has been achieved by critically reviewing the state of art on the topic under consideration, the historian needs to make clear the contribution she makes to the field. Two strategies are commonly deployed, which we also find in Sluga's and Puente Luna's works. The first is to make evident what is omitted or overlooked by other historians. For instance, Sluga points at the crucial role of women in post-Napoleonic diplomatic efforts, especially of those in the women-led salons. She also points at the importance of other non-state actors such as bankers and capitalist families, which was missed by her colleagues. Puente Luna seeks to correct the omission of Amerindians in Atlantic history, he points to the nonaristocratic visitors to the royal court that have been overlooked, and he emphasizes the need to bring power back into the analysis of the legal and imperial networks that were built.[135] The second strategy is to make clear how a particular period is misunderstood by fellow historians, or at least requires reinterpretation. One such misunderstanding mentioned by Sluga is viewing the diplomacy of the post-Napoleonic era as aimed at forcing "Europe back to its pre-revolutionary *ancien*, even cosmopolitan, past, to keep at bay a modern national future." Another misunderstanding is that "[t]he mixing of private and public is taken as the antithesis of a modern, professional culture of politics."[136] Puente Luna states that his study "allows for a reinterpretation of Andean indigenous societies during the first two centuries of Spanish rule."[137] Both strategies concern the narrative thesis, which thus once more shows its essentiality to the craft. The first strategy concerns the historical significance of actions and points directly to the narrative thesis that expresses their significance. The second strategy has to do with contrasting the thesis with competitive theses. A new thesis is meant to improve upon and hence to replace rival theses. This is how historical knowledge progresses. The second strategy does not mean that the historian contrasts statements of theses, rather the contrast is in what the thesis allows the historian – and her audience – to see in the subject under scrutiny. The

---

[134] And part of the modern concept of history as it developed at the end of the eighteenth century. See Koselleck, *Future Past*, 141 for the principle.
[135] Puente Luna, *Andean Cosmopolitans*, respectively, 6, 8, and 14.
[136] Sluga, *International Order*, 3.   [137] Puente Luna, *Andean Cosmopolitans*, 15.

diplomacy of the post-Napoleonic era in Sluga's book, as seen from her point of view, is contrasted with the diplomacy of the post-Napoleonic era as seen from a rival point of view.

Sluga frequently returns to how her work connects to that of other historians by showing how, until her work, the significance of actors is missed or misunderstood by others. Take the distinctive role of Staël, which is so important in Sluga's narrative. She ends her first chapter thus:

> [T]hrough the nineteenth and twentieth centuries, historians of diplomacy will not record diplomatic lotharios, let alone Staël's part, or the impact of women, in the critical episode of coalition formation, diplomatic negotiations, and Bonaparte's defeat. ... Instead, historians will rehearse as a matter of fact that the salon, like women's presence at all, was the antithesis of modern diplomacy. ... But in 1812, that's not what happened, at all.[138]

Note that the phrase "that's not what happened, at all" refers to what happened *under the description* of competitive narrative theses. Historians do not disagree about there being salons and the existence of the person named Germaine de Staël; they disagree about what is to be seen in them.

Her second chapter ends with noting that there are few historical commentaries on Staël's distinctive role in the coalition formation in 1812 when in Stockholm, except for those by Swedish historians. Then Sluga takes a leap to her thesis, suggesting that the significance she sees in Staël's efforts distinguishes her book from that of her fellow historians.

> For our purpose, the evidence of Staël's salon, letters, networking, and writing brings into clear, instructive view the diverse methods of diplomacy, negotiating the politics between states on the cusp of a new era. This is a history that extends beyond an exceptional woman's feelings or her ideas in the European summer of 1812. It is integral to the changing conceptions of politics more generally, whether the expanding ambitions of individual women in wartime and in anticipation of peace or the structural shifts that will position the workings of the feminine salon as the antithesis of the operations of the masculine state.[139]

Sluga *sees-in* the evidence the changing conceptions of politics, rather than inferring those conceptions from it: such is their historical significance. Because this significance is seen-in the evidence, it cannot be detached from it and hence is ingredient to it. Phrases such as "brings into clear view," "on the cusp of a new era," and "in anticipation of" are signal words with which this significance is brought to the attention of the reader. The latter two are the sort of terms typical of the narrative sentences we extensively discussed in the previous section.

---

[138] Sluga, *International Order*, 26.   [139] Sluga, *International Order*, 42.

One way to operationalize the question how histories relate is to ask: What does a new work contribute to our existing knowledge? One answer would be that it discusses newly discovered evidence. The significance of this new evidence requires it being connected to the way historians appeal to past actions and events, and hence to some narrative thesis. Another answer would be to refer to the narrative thesis itself. In the case of Sluga, the contribution consists of the thesis that the modern international order is invented in post-Napoleonic Europe. She suggests in her acknowledgments that emphasizing the importance of the period is one of the contributions she makes, and this, she adds, is done in tandem with other historians who recently did so in their own ways.[140] As we have seen, Sluga specifically makes clear the significance of women-led salons and of other non-state actors for the invention of the modern international order. The contribution is, just as in the case of Puente Luna, the book as a whole, as precisely these women and other non-state actor substantiate how she sees the invention. Mink was right when he wrote: "It is the narrative history *itself* which claims to be a contribution to knowledge."[141]

The growth of historical knowledge does not only consist of the sum of contributing individual narratives, Ankersmit notes:

> What philosophers of history often forget is that *with* and *between* all these individual contributions, a domain of generally gradually accepted historical knowledge grew up. ... it forms the background generally shared by all academic historians that enables them to understand each other.[142]

Historical knowledge is knowledge of phenomena that historians *appeal* to in order to exemplify a specific thesis. As such, these phenomena, in Ankersmit's vocabulary, instantiate models of how to conceive of them.[143] Here, clearly, historical knowledge is not to be confused with knowledge of isolated past actions and their antecedent condition. Take as an example the salons, or Staël, as something a historian appeals to in relation to, in this case, the invention of the international order. The knowledge that there were salons, or that there existed a person with the name Staël, is not the sort of knowledge Sluga teaches, except, perhaps, for novices in the field. The appeal to the salons already comes in the form of a model of how to conceive of them when students learn their craft. They might also learn about the argument that salons were sites of political influence, but the reason to appeal to the salons, including the argument, in this example, is that they exemplify the invention of the international order: That's their historical significance. Historical debate precisely concerns itself with this significance. To repeat, historians will not disagree with Sluga on

---

[140] Sluga, *International Order*, xiii–xiv.   [141] Mink, *Understanding*, 168.
[142] Ankersmit, *Representation*, 162–163.   [143] Ankersmit, *Representation*, 98–99.

the existence of salons and diplomatic efforts. Our interest here is however in narrative theses. This leaves intact of course the requirement that historians need to make plausible the claims they make about the past and support it with evidence. After Sluga's book we may appeal to salons to illustrate the "antithesis of the operations of the masculine state." Mastering these sorts of appeals is key to the historian's trade.

As Ankersmit stated, the growth of historical knowledge does not consist of the growth of individual contributions alone but also of what goes on between these contributions. According to Ankersmit, there is a common denominator among the phenomena and models they instantiate: It reflects the overall state of the art on a specific period which cannot be reduced to key single contributions.[144] Think of "the larger narrative about the formation of the Atlantic world" as the common denominator resulting from years of scholarship in which Puente Luna aims to inscribe the history he is writing. Or think of the larger narrative of nineteenth-century liberal politics in the aftermath of the Napoleonic wars as a common denominator resulting from years of scholarship in the case of Sluga's work. The evaluation of the merits of each individual narrative is made with this common denominator in mind. But the contribution that the historian offers is the thesis she proposes, which is assessed in terms of its originality, consistency, and scope, of which the latter is the most primary, as the other two depend on it.

This understanding of historical knowledge makes clear that the speed with which historical knowledge grows on a specific period usually slows down over time.[145] Puente Luna's book stimulates the growth of historical knowledge more than Sluga's book, for the simple reason that the common denominator and competing narratives available for its evaluation is slimmer compared to those of Sluga's book. This says something about the state of the art in history-writing. It does not say anything about the relative merits of these books: for that we must participate in historical debate and make use of epistemic criteria such as consistency, originality, and scope. The question what justifies preferring one work over the other is a practical, historiographical question. It has to do with the historian's interest, and, as we saw, what is missed and misunderstood by previous historians. This may concern missing the importance of gender, or agency, or the dynamics of situations going beyond the actors involved, or criticism of teleology, or criticism of nation-centrism, and so on. But only a historical discussion about these specifics justifies the choice made. Such discussion is, of course, at the very heart of the discipline, and serve to substantiate the narrative thesis one adheres to.

---

[144] Ankersmit, *Representation*, 163.   [145] Ankersmit, *Representation*, 185.

Past actions in a narrative are redescribed in terms of its thesis, which takes care of the narrative's unity and is its central message. The more the narrative's unifying message, or, as Ankersmit emphasizes, its *point of view*, adds to the action-description, the larger its *scope*, and scope-maximalization is key to narrative success.[146] Ankersmit emphasizes that scope has not to do with covering as much of the past as possible: Scope is not about *scale*. Rather, scope is about the excess or gap between what sentences state about the past and what its narrative redescription reveals. The cognitive value of a narrative vis-à-vis the cognitive value of its descriptive sentences can be measured in terms of its scope, and the wider the scope of a narrative, relative to the scope of other narratives, the better and more original it is. Sluga maximizes the scope by showing the centrality of Staël's actions, including its responses, as being integral to the invention of modern international politics. Puente Luna maximizes the scope by showing how each Andean traveler to the Habsburg court co-constructs the early modern European empire. Such scope maximalization is what narrative enables and is for.

A narrative thesis, we said, is not an empirical claim, and hence it cannot be confirmed or disconfirmed by the evidence. Rather, a thesis structures and redescribes the past actions it is concerned with. This is how the thesis functions as the ending we associate with narrative. Take the thesis that the international order was invented in post-Napoleonic Europe, or the thesis that Andean travelers co-constructed early modern Empire. If they were empirical claims, one could argue that Brook is wrong to claim that the seventeenth century was the dawn of globalization, since, as Puente Lune states, it started in the sixteenth century with the expeditions into the Inca realms. We would also be able to claim that Sluga is wrong about the international order being invented in post-Napoleonic Europe, since, first, there was no inventor doing the invention, and second, there was nothing to invent as the order already existed at least since the peace of Westphalia in 1648. But these are silly considerations that are ignorant of the nature of the theses that historians propose. The early modern European empire and the invention of the modern international order are the sorts of things that require a narrative to be intelligible, one in which historians retrace what happened, connect occurrences, and determine their significance.

David Weberman worries about Mink's claim that ingredient conclusions (narrative thesis) cannot be faulted.[147] He states: "But aside from internal

---

[146] Ankersmit, *Narrative Logic*, 237. Ankersmit, *Representation*, 50. Ankersmit also writes (*Representation*, 50, 54) that the most comprehensive narrative is able "to subsume the other in itself, and to 'explain' the others from its point of view." With the latter I agree, but I do not know how to properly understand the former.

[147] Weberman, "Saving Historical Reality," 113–138, at 124 and *passim*.

consistency, it is hard to see how narratives can be comparatively evaluated with regard to truth, accuracy, and completeness without correspondence to the touchstone of a past reality."[148] This, indeed, is hard to see for the simple reason that the complaint is circular: One cannot expect to comparatively evaluate A and B in terms of C without C (truth is accurate correspondence here). Weberman distinguishes between lenses and falsifiable theses and associates the first with Mink's ingredient conclusions. But he also seems to think that Mink would disagree with such claims as "Reagan's foreign policy ended the Cold War is more like a falsifiable thesis than like a lens."[149] Mink, however, would have no problem with taking this to be a falsifiable claim: But is it not a historical conclusion or statement of a narrative thesis, as we call them. Narrative theses are not empirical theses.[150] Since there is no evidence for a narrative thesis, no fact of the matter for it, the past reality that produced the evidence cannot function as a touchstone for its truth. I do not want to dispute the idea that new evidence may shine a new light on the past or fill in a blind spot – I get rather excited when I hear that a newly deciphered Hittite tablet sheds new light on the origin of Homer's epic. But I know that the appeal to the origin of Homer's epic already implies the sort of conception of the event that is associated with narrative. I also do not want to dispute the idea that historians can and should correct myths and other false stories about the past and the misuse of it.[151] But our interest here is in the narrative theses that historians propose, rather than in their (important) capacity of speakers of truth to power. Narrative theses are evaluated in terms of consistency and scope, and, as the example of Sluga shows, their validity depends not the past and its remains, but on what they allow us to see in the past and its remains on the one hand, and their connection to other theses on the other.

A thesis allows for internal consistency, but each historical narrative also needs to be consistent with other narratives in a sense to be explained. As the example of Sluga shows, she herself positions her thesis vis-à-vis competing theses. The touchstone here is not past reality or its remains. Rather, the thesis is

---

[148] Weberman, "Saving Historical Reality," 127. See also Weberman, "Saving Historical Reality," 129–130.
[149] Weberman, "Saving Historical Reality," 125.
[150] Cf. Currie, "Narratives," 265–287, at 274, who writes that Mink would insist that the claim that "Churchill's love of animals matters because it led to his desiring a platypus" cannot be true or false. Mink however would obviously see this as something to be true or false. Critics of Mink usually present empirical claims to make clear that theses can be confirmed or disconfirmed, adding that evidence, and the archival work connected to it, proves or disproves the claims that historians make, as Currie, "Narratives," 283, for example has it. But this is not something Mink would deny. He has something else in mind.
[151] Jo Guldi and David Armitage emphasize this throughout, with well-chosen examples, in their *The History Manifesto*.

seen-in the remains and the actions and events that can be inferred from them, and as such, a thesis *precedes* what is to count as a touchstone. A thesis may *misrepresent* the past in the specific sense connected to this. In Sluga's view, the competitive theses misrepresent diplomatic actions, that is, they fail to properly see-in diplomatic actions what their historical significance is and fail to properly present a synoptic vision of the period under consideration. Here misrepresentation does not concern the action, or the evidence from which the action can be inferred, but their redescription in terms of the narrative thesis. This distinction is crucial. Theses can be rationally discussed in terms of epistemic criteria such as coherence, consistency, originality, and scope. And their acceptance does not require the past or its remains as a touchstone. Accepting Sluga's narrative means assenting with the statements she makes in her narrative. If the narrative improves our understanding of post-Napoleonic diplomacy vis-à-vis its rivals that we are already familiar with, by being more comprehensive, that is, in terms of the synoptic mastery it allows, and *replaces* them, then her narrative is considered to be the best guide to the past present at hand.

What causes a narrative to be replaced by another? The main reason is that the historians' interests and concerns change over time and hence have a history themselves: New questions arise as the sociopolitical context in which historians' works change. The answers a narrative provides needs to be in line with the demands for the narrative in its specific context. New interests and questions lead to new significance, which correctness depends on the narrative as a whole, since the narrative as a whole is the justification of the thesis it expresses, which includes connecting it to competing (statements of) theses. The acceptance of the narrative thesis that the international order was invented in post-Napoleonic Europe depends on the narrative itself.

3.5 Narrative Reason

A thesis is a knowledge claim, albeit not an empirical claim; rather it presents the background of the empirical claims made in a narrative. But since it is a knowledge claim, it is something that the historian is responsible for: When asked, she needs to be able to give reasons for it. This *normative* character of knowing is emphasized by the neo-Kantian Wilfrid Sellars:

> The essential point is that in characterizing an episode or a state as that of *knowing*, we are not giving an empirical description of that episode or state; we are placing it in the logical space of reasons, of justifying and being able to justify what one says.[152]

---

[152] Sellars, "Empiricism and the Philosophy of Mind," 169 (§36).

A historian needs to be able to justify both her empirical claims and her thesis. When asked why Andeans traveled to the Spanish Court, Puente Luna would give the answer: To seek justice and reward, and when further pressed, he would offer the evidence for it and present the sort of practical reasoning at work in the explanation of action. Thus, he justifies the empirical claim. If we ask him: Why do we need to know that? The answer would be: because of its historical significance, as the Andeans co-constructed the early modern empire. When asked to justify the thesis that Andeans co-constructed early modern empire, he would present his narrative, which *is* the justification of it.[153] The historian does not so much give reasons for her thesis, as there is no evidence for or against it, rather, the thesis is the reason given for past actions and events (as inferred from the evidence) having the historical significance they have, and why they are described in terms of the thesis. When Sluga is asked why she describes Staël's salons the way she does in her book, she will refer to her thesis, not to empirical evidence. A narrative thesis is seen in the evidence and what can be inferred from it, and hence it precedes the narrative's descriptions and explanations.

The Kantian origin of the logical space of reason that Sellars talks about reminds us that this space is an *ideal space* with a *regulatory* function, without any definite descriptive content. We already pointed at the specificity of it in the case of the discipline of history, where the narrative is the justification for the thesis it proposes, and the thesis the reason for the past having the historical significance it has. As the two historiographical examples showed, each in their own way, narrative theses are connected to other narratives. The relation between historical narratives is best understood in terms of the *requirement of external consistency*, which is, as a requirement, an *intellectual demand* typical of the ideal order that governs the discipline. Simply put, we require of the historian to be able to explain how her work connects to and improves upon the work of their peers, and for that they rely on the narrative thesis they propose. This returns us to Mink's unresolved dilemma: "narrative histories should be aggregative, insofar as they are histories, but cannot be, insofar as they are narratives." They cannot aggregate since a narrative, qua narrative, "must have a unity of its own."[154] The unity of a narrative, we said throughout this Element, results from the thesis proposed by the historian. A thesis may replace another thesis, and a thesis may be explained from the point of view of another thesis, but they do not aggregate. As histories, the dilemma states, narratives should be aggregative, this is so because all history presupposes to be concerned with the

---

[153] As Ankersmit, *Representation*, 179, writes: "if a historian was asked what their arguments were for defending a certain thesis and, replied 'just read the book again,' this would be an entirely appropriate and adequate response to the question." See also Mink, *Understanding*, 198.
[154] Mink, *Understanding*, 197.

same and "single determinate realm" we call the past.[155] The requirement of external consistency needs to allow for both aggregation and non-aggregation at the same time if it is to resolve the dilemma. The difficulty is to have a proper sense of the presupposition mentioned. Mink proposes to abandon it, but this does not solve his dilemma.[156] The dilemma he sees connects to the correlative dilemma suggesting that histories are rationally evaluable inasmuch as they are forms of empirical inquiry, whereas they are not inasmuch as they are narratives.[157] To resolve Mink's dilemma, we need to see the presupposition for what it is: an intellectual demand that is part of the historian's trade.

One way to think of consistency between narratives is in terms of what Ankersmit calls the common denominator that comes along with and between the proliferation of historical narratives. When Puente Luna aims to inscribe his narrative in the larger narrative of the Atlantic world, he has this common denominator in mind: the knowledge that historians have produced about the Atlantic world in the early modern period and of which he is aware. His work is consistent with other narratives in terms of the common denominator that historians, including himself, together establish. Here the common denominator serves as a standard to determine how valuable contribution to historical knowledge the monograph is.[158] This is one horn of Mink's dilemma. Consistency here is being able as a historian, and as a reader of their work, to situate a narrative in the field regarding a specific subject. It is nothing more than being able to classify narratives in terms of their relation to other narratives: narratives on the early modern Atlantic world, or the Habsburg dynasty, or on modern international relations. Histories, in this specific sense, aggregate, as they widen and define the field as they are being written. However, when historians situate their work in the field, as we have seen, they have something else and more important in mind then merely (re-)establishing some common denominator, which is, after all, a by-product of their work rather than their contribution itself: They want to improve on existing accounts, and they do so with their narrative thesis, which is unique, embodied by the narrative, and having a unity of its own – that is how they contribute to historical knowledge. Here the requirement of consistency is still in place, of course, but the standard of what counts as contribution is not the common denominator but the comprehensiveness and originality of its thesis, that is, its scope. Since narratives have a unity of their own, they do not aggregate. That is the other horn of Mink's

---

[155] Mink, *Understanding*, 197.
[156] Mink, *Understanding*, 202. For a discussion of it, see Van den Akker, "Mink's Riddle of Narrative Truth," 346–370.
[157] Roth, "Back to the Future," 270–281, at 271.   [158] Ankersmit, *Representation*, 164.

dilemma. Formulated as this, the dilemma resolves in that the one horn does not conflict with the other.

The requirement of external consistency is a methodological principle. It demands of historians to connect their thesis to other theses and improve on them. Historians need to situate their work in the history of history-writing and more specifically its current state of the art. This history of history-writing in turn makes use of the notion of there being *one historical world*, which is presumed in the idea of histories being consistent and in there being a common denominator of historical knowledge that results from the proliferation of historical accounts. This notion of the one historical world, Gallie argues, is not the empirical ground that allows for histories to be consistent with one another:

> [T]he relation between the one historical world and the requirement of consistency as between different histories is not that of ground and consequent, ... but rather that of mutual entailment between two distinct yet necessarily connected notions.[159]

The one historical world, Gallie holds, is an intellectual ideal: "an idea without any definite descriptive content, indeed it is not an empirical idea at all." It is rather "a Kantian ideal of reason," with a regulatory function.[160] The requirement of histories being mutually consistent, Gallie continues, is "a logician's formal statement of an *intellectual demand*."[161] This intellectual demand for mutual consistency is *productive* in that it compels historians to connect their accounts to others in the sense that we have given it: inscribing the work in the history of history-writing, improve on competitive theses, and maximize the scope of their thesis, relative to present day interests and concerns. Remember the example of Sluga. Her thesis conflicts with the one that takes the "mixing of private and public ... as the antithesis of a modern, professional culture of politics." There is a conflict not in terms of what happened, but in terms of the significance of what occurred, in what is seen-in what transpired and in the evidence it left behind.

Let us return to Mink's dilemma. Narratives do not aggregate, but histories do in that each individual account needs to be situated in the history of history-writing and self-consciously contribute to it in terms of its thesis, and, as a byproduct, in terms of the common denominator that with and between accounts comes into existence. This is what the requirement of consistency,

---

[159] Gallie, *Philosophy*, 58–59. Gallie discusses a passage from Collingwood which, I think, together with Gallie's discussion, informed Mink's dilemma. Ankersmit discusses the requirement and refers to it as the "presumption of consistency" in his *Representation*, 166–167, 177, 196.
[160] Gallie, *Philosophy*, 59.   [161] Gallie, *Philosophy*, 60.

which is an intellectual demand, captures, and here the rationality of the discipline is to be situated. Situating one's work in the history of history-writing is partaking in the space of reasons.

Let me conclude.

The past or its remains does not serve as touchstone as to what narrative is to be preferred. The narrative itself provides the justification for the thesis it proposes. Accepting a narrative thesis is accepting the statements made possible by it in the narrative. This thesis is meant to improve upon rival theses, and this is determined in terms of criteria such as originality, consistency, and scope. Scope maximalization is what historians should strive for. The discipline requires of each genuine historical work that it is consistent with other works. This is not an empirical matter, but an intellectual demand, and as such part of the space of reasons in which the historian, as a producer of knowledge, operates. The thesis *is* the reason for past actions and events having the historical significance they have.

Narrativist philosophers of history such as Gallie, Danto, and Mink give up on the idea of the past as a "determinate realm of unchanging reality." This does not mean, as Mink has it, that:

> there is nothing determinate about the past, since individual statements of fact, of the sort to which so much historical research is dedicated, remain unaffected. But it does mean that the significance of the past is determinate only by virtue of our own disciplined imagination. Insofar as the significance of past occurrences is understandable only as they are locatable in the ensemble of interrelationships that can be grasped only in the construction of narrative form, it is we who make the past determinate in that respect.[162]

The disciplined imagination that Mink refers to is what we in this Element referred to as the narrative thesis. It is up to historians to determine the significance of the past, which means, among other things, and as Danto concludes in his classic work, that "history is made by them."[163]

Epilogue

This Element is concerned with narrative as a mode of knowing. Narratives, we argued, make the past intelligible to us, as they allow us to see actions in temporal perspective, affording practical knowledge. Much attention has been given to the theses that historians propose, which redescribe the actions and events they are concerned with in terms of it and thus allow for a narrative's unity. These theses, we argued, are indispensable and qualify the work of historians as narrative.

---

[162] Mink, *Understanding*, 202.   [163] Danto, *Narration*, 284.

The interest in narrative is often motivated by the question how history as a discipline is different from the natural and social sciences.[164] This was especially so when the interest in narrative arose in the 1960s and became central in the debates in the philosophy of history, but it still motivates scholars in our day.[165] At that time, the change within the philosophy of history from attending to the logic of explanation to the logic of narrative coincided with the divergence of history and sociology after their convergence under the banner of the deductive nomological model of explanation.[166] Narrative came to be what makes the historian stand out among her fellow academics. There is no need to elaborate on this initial motivation here, but I do want to express my agreement with Danto's position which, I think, still holds:

> A certain autonomy then attaches to history, indeed to narrative history, which cannot become more 'scientific' without losing its defining human importance since it is human interests, after all, which determine which events are important and under what sort of description.[167]

This passage suggests that it is not the narrative per se which sets history apart, but the human interests with which the historian starts her work. The importance of the historian's interest in connection to narrative and the sort of description that narrative allows have been central in this Element. Throughout we emphasized that asking for the historical significance of an event leads the historian to the narrative thesis she proposes, which ensures the coherence of her narrative. This thesis is specific to narrative and different from the sort of empirical thesis or conclusion one finds in the sciences. So history as a discipline does stand out by relying on narrative. This is not to deny that historians study past remains, carefully describe what occurred, develop arguments, and device explanations. But these scientific activities all serve the thesis they propose, which is the "soul" of the historian's narrative.

The concern with narrative has not lost any of its relevance, for the simple reason that it informs us about history as an academic discipline and the knowledge it produces. For as long as historians decide what events in their past are important and for what reason, they will rely on narrative. Pleading for a pre-narrativist or post-narrativist philosophy of history therefore is ill-conceived

---

[164] For overviews of what is known as *narrativism*, see Roberts, "Introduction," 1–21, Kuukkanen, *Postnarrativist*, 1–29, and Tozzi, "Narrativism," 113–128. Ricoeur provides a helpful summary and discussion of several of the key authors and issues of the 1960s and 1970s in his *Time*, 121ff.

[165] See for instance Roth, *Structure*. I expressed my agreement with Danto's position quoted below in my *Exemplifying Past*, 20.

[166] See the essay by Mink, "The Divergence of History and Sociology in Recent Philosophy of History," in his *Understanding*, 163–181.

[167] Danto, *Narration*, xii.

Knowledge and Narrative 55

inasmuch as it ignores the narrative and the specificity of its thesis or makes a caricature of it.[168]

In the previous section, we noted that Mink left open the crucial questions why narratives are accepted, how they are logically compared, and on what grounds one is preferred over the other. These questions have been taken up more recently by such diverse scholars as Jouni-Matti Kuukkanen, Paul Roth, and Frank Ankersmit, and they have been our concern in this Element as well. The thesis *is* the reason for the past having the historical significance it has, and the narrative *is* the justification of its thesis. A thesis needs to be comprehensive, consistent, and having a scope as wide as possible. The requirement to maximalize the scope of the thesis and the requirements of internal and external consistency are intellectual demands that are central to history as a trade. Mastering these demands puts one into the ranks of historians. In the previous section, much attention has been given to the second requirement, as it is the one that is easily misunderstood. The thesis that historians propose are not empirical theses, though the narratives in which they feature need to be consistent with other works of history, as all history is consistent with itself, that is, concerned with the one historical world. This one historical world is not the empirical past nor a description of it, but a regulative ideal that guides the work of historians and the corollary of the notion of the consistency of histories.

Criticism of the interest in narrative traditionally has been twofold. One is that it distracts attention from historical research and the epistemological problems associated with it. Here the point is that the evidence studied by the historian is central to the discipline as it supports the claims they make and hence the truth of what they state. A second complaint is that it allegedly disregards the antecedent conditions of actions by centering on actions and events as central to narrative.[169] Both criticisms are not well founded, but this did not stop them from being raised time and again. As to the second complaint: The interest in narrative does not imply passing over the conditions leading to actions and events, their developments and changes because of it, as the antecedent conditions of actions and its consequences, intended and unintended, are part of the very concept of action. This we have emphasized several times throughout this Element. As to the first complaint: Attending to one issue does not dismiss or deny the relevance of the other. More importantly, there is

---

[168] The postnarrativism argued for by Kuukkanen follows from misleadingly opposing the historian as critical reasoner to that of a storyteller (*Postnarrativist*, 67), the erroneous association of narratives with "just a set of descriptions of singular events" (87, see also 91), and the false statement that narrative form implies that "historians have to present their works temporally or chronologically" (88, see also 92 and 96). See also Rogacz, "Unheeded History," 474–489. Cf. n95.

[169] Mink, *Understanding*, 177–178.

no contradiction in the view that evidence supports the historian's statements about the past and the view that a narrative thesis, from a logical point of view, *precedes* these statements while itself not being supported by the evidence but seen-in the evidence. In Section 2, we gave statements on the past their due.

From the outset of this Element, we have emphasized that narrative is concerned with the field of action, with the sort of intelligibility that is associated with *praxis* rather than with *theoria*.[170] Practical wisdom, *phronēsis*, is "the intelligent use of action," as Ricoeur puts it.[171] This practical wisdom, in the case of the discipline of history, derives from the thesis that historians propose, as the examples discussed in this Element showed. This thesis, seen-in the actions studied by the historian, structures and redescribes those actions in terms of it, giving the sequence of events the unity we associate with narrative. As so often, Mink was right in what must be his first essay in the philosophy of history: Historians *are* "wiser than they can say, but only if we hear what they have to tell."[172]

---

[170] The connection between history being concerned with the field of action and the wisdom it affords also seems what Gallie has in mind in his *Philosophy*, 130–139.

[171] Ricoeur, *Time*, 40.   [172] Mink, *Understanding*, 86. The essay was published in 1966.

Bibliography

Ahlskog, Jonas, "Pre-narrativist Philosophy of History," *Journal of the Philosophy of History*, 17:2 (2023), 195–218.

Ahlskog, Jonas and Giuseppina D'Oro, "Beyond Narrativism: The Historical Past and Why It Can Be Known," *Collingwood and British Idealism Studies*, 27:1 (2021), 5–33.

Ankersmit, Frank, *Narrative Logic: A Semantic Analysis of the Historian's Language*, Meppel: Krips Repro, 1981.

Ankersmit, Frank, *Representation: The Birth of Historical Reality from the Death of the Past*, New York: Columbia University Press, 2024.

Aristotle, *Poëtica*, Trans. N. van der Ben and J. M. Bremer, Amsterdam: Athenaeum, Polak & Van Gennep, 1995.

Assis, Arthur Alfaix, *Plural Pasts: Historiography between Events and Structures. Cambridge Elements in Historical Theory and Practice*, Cambridge: Cambridge University Press, 2023.

Assis, Alfaix, "Shapes and Functions of Historical Events," *Rethinking History*, online April 22, 2025.

Ayer, Alfred J., "Statements about the Past," *Philosophical Essays*, London: Macmillan, 1969 [1954].

Brook, Timothy, *Vermeer's Hat: The Seventeenth Century and the Dawn of the Global World*, London: Profile Books, 2008.

Carr, David, *Time, Narrative, and History*, Indianapolis: Bloomington, 1986.

Currie, Adrian, "Narratives, Events & Monotremes: The Philosophy of History in Practice," *Journal of the Philosophy of History*, 17:2 (2023), 265–287.

Danto, Arthur, *Narration and Knowledge*, New York: Columbia University Press, 1985.

Davidson, Donald, "Agency," in *Essays on Actions and Events*, Oxford: Clarendon Press, 2013, 45–46.

Davidson, Donald, *Essays on Actions and Events*, Oxford: Clarendon Press, 2013 [2001].

Davidson, Donald, *Truth and Predication*, Cambridge, MA: Harvard University Press, 2005.

Dray, William H., "On the Nature and Role of Narrative in History," in Geoffrey Roberts ed., *The History and Narrative Reader*, London and New York: Routledge, 2001, 25–39.

Dummett, Michael, *Truth and Other Enigmas*, London: Duckworth, 1978.

Dummett, Michael, *Truth and the Past*, New York: Columbia University Press, 2004.

Dyke, Heather, "Time and Tense," in Heather Dyke and Adrian Bardon eds., *A Companion to the Philosophy of Time*, Chichester: Wiley-Blackwell, 2013, 328–343.

Gallie, Walter B., *Philosophy and the Historical Understanding*, 2nd Ed. New York: Schocken Books, 1968.

Goldie, Peter, *The Mess Inside: Narrative, Emotion, & the Mind*, Oxford: Oxford University Press, 2012.

Goodman, Nelson, *Language of Art: An Approach to a Theory of Symbols*, Indianapolis: Hackett, 1976.

Guldi, Jo and David Armitage's, *The History Manifesto*, Cambridge: Cambridge University Press, 2014.

Imaz-Sheinbaum, Mariana, *Historical Narratives: Constructable, Evaluable, Inevitable*, London: Routledge, 2024.

Koselleck, Reinhart, *Futures Past: On the Semantics of Historical Times*, New York: Columbia University Press, 2004.

Kuukkanen, Jouni-Matti, *Postnarrativist Philosophy of Historiography*, Hampshire: Palgrave Macmillan, 2015.

MacIntyre, Alasdair, *After Virtue*, London: Bloomsbury, 2007 [1981].

Megill, Allan, "Recounting the Past: Description, Explanation, and Narrative in Historiography," *The American Historical Review*, 94:3 (1989), 627–653.

Mink, Louis O., "The Divergence of History and Sociology in Recent Philosophy of History," in *Historical Understanding*, 163–181.

Mink, Louis O., *Historical Understanding*, eds. Brian Fay, Eugene O. Golob, and Richard T. Vann, Ithaca and London: Cornell University Press, 1987.

Olafson, Frederick A., "Narrative History and the Concept of Action," *History and Theory*, 9:3 (1970), 265–289.

Puckett, Kent, *Narrative Theory: A Critical Introduction*. Cambridge: Cambridge University Press, 2016.

Puente Luna, José Carlos de la, *Andean Cosmopolitans: Seeking Justice and Reward at the Spanish Royal Court*, Austin: University of Texas Press, 2018.

Ricoeur, Paul, *Time and Narrative*. Vol I, Chicago: The University of Chicago Press, 1984.

Roberts Geoffrey, "Introduction: The History and Narrative Debate, 1960–2000," in Roberts ed., *The History and Narrative Reader*, London: Routledge, 2001, 1–21.

Rogacz, Dawid, "Unheeded History: A Critical Engagement with Jouni-Matti Kuukkanen's 'postnarrativism'," *Rethinking History*, 22:4 (2018), 474–489.

Roth, Paul A., "Back to the Future: Postnarrativist Historiography and the Analytical Philosophy of History," *History and Theory*, 55:2 (2016), 270–281, at 271.

Roth, Paul. A., *The Philosophical Structure of Historical Explanation*, Evanston: Northwestern University Press, 2020.

Sellars, Wilfrid, "Empiricism and the Philosophy of Mind," in *Science, Perception and Reality*, Atascadero: Ridgeview, 1991 [1963], 169 (§36).

Sellars, Wilfrid, *Science, Perception and Reality*, Atascadero: Ridgeview, 1991 [1963].

Skinner, Quentin, "Meaning and Understanding," in *Visions of Politics. Vol. I. Regarding Method*, Cambridge: Cambridge University Press, 2006 [2002], 77.

Skinner, Quentin, *Visions of Politics. Vol.I Regarding Method*, Cambridge: Cambridge University Press, 2006 [2002].

Sluga, Glenda, *The Invention of the International Order: Remaking Europe after Napoleon*, Princeton: Princeton University Press, 2021.

Tozzi, Verónica, "Narrativism," in Chiel van den Akker, ed., *The Routledge Companion to Historical Theory*, London: Routledge, 2022, 113–128.

Van den Akker, Chiel, "Mink's Riddle of Narrative Truth," *Journal of the Philosophy of History*, 7:3 (2013), 346–370.

Van den Akker, Chiel, *The Exemplifying Past: A Philosophy of History*, Amsterdam: Amsterdam University Press, 2018.

Van den Akker, Chiel, *The Modern Idea of History and Its Value: An Introduction*. Amsterdam: Amsterdam University Press, 2020.

Velleman, J. David, "Narrative Explanation," *The Philosophical Review*, 112:1 (2003), 1–25.

Weberman, David, "Saving Historical Reality (Even if We Construct It)," in Tor Egil Førland and Branko Mitrović eds., *The Poverty of Anti-realism: Critical Perspectives on Postmodernist Philosophy of History*, Lanham: Lexington Books, 2023, 113–138.

White, Hayden, *Tropics of Discourse: Essays in Cultural Criticism*, Baltimore: The Johns Hopkins University Press, 1978.

White, Hayden, *The Content of the Form: Narrative Discourse and Historical Representation*, Baltimore: The Johns Hopkins University Press, 1987.

Williams, Bernard, "Another Time, Another Place, Another Person," in *Moral Luck*. Philosophical Papers 1973–1980. Cambridge: Cambridge University Press, 1997 [1981], 164–173.

Williams, Bernard, "Life as Narrative," *European Journal of Philosophy*, 17:2 (2007), 305–317.

Williams, Bernard, *Shame and Necessity*, Berkeley: University of California Press, 2008 [1993].

Zeleňák, Eugen, "Two Versions of a Constructivist View of Historical Work," *History and Theory*, 54 (2015), 209–225.

Zeleňák, Eugen, "Representation," in Chiel van den Akker ed., *The Routledge Companion to Historical Theory*, London: Routledge, 2022, 299–315.

Acknowledgment

I would like to thank Allan Megill, Frank Ankersmit, and the editor Daniel Woolf for their comments on a previous version of this Element. I also thank two anonymous reviewers for their positive reviews and suggestions.

Historical Theory and Practice

Daniel Woolf
Queen's University, Ontario

Daniel Woolf is Professor of History at Queen's University, where he served for ten years as Principal and Vice-Chancellor, and has held academic appointments at a number of Canadian universities. He is the author or editor of several books and articles on the history of historical thought and writing, and on early modern British intellectual history, including most recently *A Concise History of History* (CUP 2019). He is a Fellow of the Royal Historical Society, the Royal Society of Canada, and the Society of Antiquaries of London. He is married with three adult children.

Editorial Board

Dipesh Chakrabarty, *University of Chicago*
Marnie Hughes-Warrington, *University of South Australia*
Ludmilla Jordanova, *University of Durham*
Angela McCarthy, *University of Otago*
María Inés Mudrovcic, *Universidad Nacional de Comahue*
Herman Paul, *Leiden University*
Stefan Tanaka, *University of California, San Diego*
Richard Ashby Wilson, *University of Connecticut*

About the Series

Cambridge Elements in Historical Theory and Practice is a series intended for a wide range of students, scholars, and others whose interests involve engagement with the past. Topics include the theoretical, ethical, and philosophical issues involved in doing history, the interconnections between history and other disciplines and questions of method, and the application of historical knowledge to contemporary global and social issues such as climate change, reconciliation and justice, heritage, and identity politics.

Cambridge Elements

Historical Theory and Practice

Elements in the Series

Conceptualizing the History of the Present Time
María Inés Mudrovcic

Writing the History of the African Diaspora
Toyin Falola

Dealing with Dark Pasts: A European History of Auto-Critical Memory in Global Perspective
Itay Lotem

A Human Rights View of the Past
Antoon De Baets

Historians' Autobiographies as Historiographical Inquiry: A Global Perspective
Jaume Aurell

Historiographic Reasoning
Aviezer Tucker

Pragmatism and Historical Representation
Serge Grigoriev

History and Hermeneutics
Paul Fairfield

Testimony and Historical Knowledge: Authority, Evidence and Ethics in Historiography
Jonas Ahlskog

Contested Public Monuments: Global perspectives on landscapes of memory
Maria Grever

Things of the Past: A Modern Yearning
Kasper Risbjerg Eskildsen

Knowledge and Narrative
Chiel van den Akker

A full series listing is available at: www.cambridge.org/EHTP

For EU product safety concerns, contact us at Calle de José Abascal, 56–1°, 28003 Madrid, Spain or eugpsr@cambridge.org.

www.ingramcontent.com/pod-product-compliance
Lightning Source LLC
LaVergne TN
LVHW011857060526
838200LV00054B/4395